Critical Bibliographies in Modern History

Nineteenth-Century
Britain
1815–1914

Critical Bibliographies in Modern History

Nineteenth-Century Britain 1815–1914

DAVID NICHOLLS
Lecturer in History, Manchester Polytechnic

DAWSON · ARCHON BOOKS

First published in 1978

© D. Nicholls 1978

All rights reserved. No part of this publication may be reproduced, stored in a retrieval system, or transmitted, in any form or by any means, electronic, mechanical, photocopying, recording or otherwise without the permission of the publishers:

Wm Dawson & Son Ltd, Cannon House
Folkestone, Kent, England

Archon Books, The Shoe String Press, Inc.
995 Sherman Avenue, Hamden
Connecticut 06514 USA

British Library Cataloguing in Publication Data

Nicholls, David
   Nineteenth-century Britain, 1815–1914—
   (Critical bibliographies in modern history).
   1. Great Britain—History—19th century—
   Bibliography
   I. Title   II. Series
   016.941081   Z2019

ISBN 0-7129-0825-0

Archon ISBN 0 208 01730 5

Printed in Great Britain
by W & J Mackay Limited, Chatham

For mum and dad

CONTENTS

PREFACE		*page* 11
1	GENERAL	17
2	POLITICAL AND CONSTITUTIONAL	23
	General	24
	Monarchy	28
	Central government and administration	29
	The electoral system	31
	(a) General	31
	(b) The Reform Acts	33
	(c) Electoral finance	33
	(d) Women's suffrage	34
	(e) Elections	34
	(f) Local politics	34
	Parliament	35
	Political parties	36
	(a) General	36
	(b) Conservatism	37
	(c) Liberalism	38
	(d) Radicalism	39
	(e) Labour	40
	Political thought	44
	Political biography	45
	Local government	54
3	FOREIGN, IMPERIAL AND DEFENCE	56
	Foreign policy	56
	(a) General	56
	(b) Monographs	58
	(c) Practitioners	58
	Imperialism	59
	(a) Theories	59
	(b) General	60
	(c) Monographs	62

	Defence	*page* 63
	(a) General	63
	(b) The army	64
	(c) The navy	64
4	ECONOMIC	66
	General	67
	Agriculture	70
	Industry	72
	(a) General	72
	(b) Coal mining	73
	(c) Cotton during the famine	73
	(d) Newspapers	73
	(e) Industrial archaeology	74
	Overseas trade and investment	75
	Transport	76
	(a) General	76
	(b) Railways	77
	Trade unions and labour relations	78
5	SOCIAL	82
	General	83
	Population	87
	Rural society	91
	(a) General	91
	(b) The landed classes	91
	(c) The village labourer	92
	Urban society	93
	(a) The middle classes	93
	(b) The working classes	94
	(c) Class relationships	96
	(d) Working-class movements	98
	The status of women	101
	Children	102
	Sexuality	103
	Leisure	104
	Social reform	104
	(a) General	104
	(b) Poverty and the Poor Law	106
	(c) Factory legislation	109
	(d) Public health	109

	(e) Anti-slavery	page 110
	(f) Crime and punishment	111
	(g) Temperance	112
	(h) Housing	113
	Urban history	113
	(a) General	113
	(b) A note on books on particular towns	115
	(c) Photographic collections	115
6	EDUCATION	117
	General	118
	(a) History	118
	(b) Theory	119
	Elementary and secondary	120
	Public schools	122
	Universities	123
	Technical education	124
	Adult education	124
7	RELIGION	126
	General	126
	The Church of England	128
	Evangelicalism	129
	The Oxford Movement	129
	Roman Catholicism	130
	Nonconformity	130
	The churches and social reform	132
8	WALES, SCOTLAND AND IRELAND	134
	General	135
	Wales	135
	(a) General	135
	(b) Political	135
	(c) Economic	135
	(d) Social	136
	Scotland	137
	(a) General	137
	(b) Political	137
	(c) Economic	138
	(d) Social	139
	(e) Religion	140

Ireland	*page*	141
(a) General		141
(b) Political		142
(c) Economic		145
(d) Social		146
(e) Religion		148

9 LITERARY AND CULTURAL — 149

APPENDIX A Addenda — 153
B A Guide to Periodical Literature — 157

INDEX OF AUTHORS — 163

PREFACE

More has probably been written about Britain in the nineteenth century than about any other period in her history. Some idea of the vast quantity of material now available can be gauged from the tens of thousands of entries in the recent Oxford bibliographies.[1] But while these compilations are invaluable for the research student, the average history student in secondary schools, colleges, polytechnics and universities will find them merely intimidating. It is for this admittedly hypothetical 'average student' and the general reader with a keen interest in nineteenth-century British history that the present bibliography is written.

Every teacher of history must at some time or other have been confronted with the question, 'Which book do you recommend I buy?', and, faced with an enormous number of books which ostensibly deal with the same subject, the student is entitled to some sort of guidance. Historians have been strangely reluctant to proffer that guidance—at least in book-form. Critical bibliographies are therefore few and far between. Those which do exist either devote only part of their space to the nineteenth century, or are too short to be of great service. And all of them are now dated.[2] The present bibliography is therefore a considered selection of the multitude of books on nineteenth-century Britain in the English language that are available. Selection and critical appraisal are inevitably matters of personal judgement,

---

[1] L. M. Brown and I. R. Christie (eds.), *Bibliography of British history 1789–1851* (1977); H. J. Hanham (ed.), *Bibliography of British history 1851–1914* (1976). Shorter handlists are J. L. Altholz (ed.), *Victorian England 1837–1901* (1970) and A. F. Havighurst (ed.), *Modern England 1901–70* (1976) published by Cambridge University Press, but the first, which covers the bulk of our period, is a little out of date. W. H. Chaloner and R. C. Richardson (comps.), *British economic and social history. A bibliographical guide* (1976) is useful within its chosen fields, but it does contain more than its fair share of inaccuracies. These books are not critical bibliographies, though they include the occasional throwaway comments. There are, in addition, a number of annual bibliographical lists—see, for example, those published by the Royal Historical Society (currently under the editorial direction of G. R. Elton), the Historical Association, and by certain periodicals (see Appendix B).

[2] See G. R. Elton, *Modern historians on British history 1485–1945: a critical bibliography 1945–69* (1970); E. C. Furber (ed.), *Changing views on British history. Essays on historical writing since 1939* (1966); and the Historical Association pamphlet by I. R. Christie, *British history since 1760; a select bibliography* (1970).

and the compiler is inclined to feel both apologetic and defensive for his winnowing. I was, however, assisted in my choice of mainstream books by the response to my request for reading-lists from the History departments of universities and polytechnics in the United Kingdom. Those lists helped to clarify for me the type of material which is currently in most common use at undergraduate-level, and, I hope, suppressed some of my own prejudices. I would like to take this opportunity to thank all those who took the trouble to reply.

At the present time, the most encouraging development in nineteenth-century British historiography is the belated but nonetheless welcome appearance of a growing number of studies which have their basis in social theory. The massive imbalance between theoretical and empirical history is at last slowly being rectified. But much of our reading (and, indeed, teaching) still remains firmly embedded in the liberal tradition, and the contents of this bibliography reflect that fact. I have not worked on the principle of excluding all that I dislike or consider bad history. For example, I am not enamoured of many of the collections of short documentary extracts which are on the market, but I am conscious of the fact that many teachers do find them useful, and I have tried to do justice to them. Also, much bad popular history is so easily available that I have felt it a duty to deflect the unwary from it. Rather, the type of material most readily rejected was the antiquarian and outdated, books either too recondite or too specialised for our 'average student', and material which was not generally accessible. In sum, I hope that I have included all the most important books that our average reader is likely to encounter and that the end-product is a serviceable guide for both student and teacher.

The bibliography is arranged into the conventional compartments—political, economic, social, and so on. Such a division is never, of course, entirely satisfactory but I hope that at least some of the usual obstacles have been surmounted by the incorporation of cross-referencing and an author-index to entries. It will be seen from a quick glance at the contents that the bulk of the entries are in two of the sections—political and constitutional, and social—and this reflects the current state of nineteenth-century British historiography. The study of high politics has for some time given way to a preoccupation with social history, but it reigned for so long and trained sufficient disciples to ensure a respectable annual output of new work. It is in the field of social history, however, that much the most interesting work has appeared in the last two decades, and the subdivisions of this particular branch of history are likely to continue to expand for some time to come.

The problem of periodisation which confronts all historians creates particular difficulties for the bibliographer. Not only is the chosen time-span an artificial one (though 1815–1914 is popular with history teachers, sandwiched as it is between two major European conflagrations), but the wide range of subjects encompassed by a bibliography does not fit neatly into it. The problem is, however, reduced to a degree by the fact that this book is one volume in a continuing series. In anticipation of this I have generally excluded those books whose weight lies outside the chosen period, or which deal with Britain only as a part of European or global history.

Original dates of publication have been given throughout as the age of a book is often, though not always, a clue to the quality and style of its contents, but not the place of publication, a convention the advantage of which I have never quite been able to fathom. Indeed the general reader is likely to follow up the details in this bibliography in one of two ways—either by tracing a particular book through a library-catalogue or by purchasing it—and in both eventualities the information presented here is sufficient. Books currently on the market, and information as to their availability in paperback in different countries, can, for example, be readily traced through such publications as the annual *British books in print* or in North America in *Books in print*. This last factor also accounts for the omission of any reference to the publishers of each book who will be different according to country of purchase, the particular edition of the book, its type of cover (hardback or paperback), and so on. I have, however, included as far as possible the publication-date of the latest edition of any particular book where it has been revised or updated.

The introductions to each section present a review of current trends in that particular branch of history and of some of the glaring gaps in our knowledge that remain to be plugged. There, and occasionally in the individual entries, I have also alluded, either by reference to subject or author, to certain books which were deemed too specialised for inclusion in a bibliography of this sort. To have appended full details would have entailed an unnecessary lengthening of this basic guide, particularly as most of these books can easily be traced in the Oxford bibliographies or the catalogues of books in print referred to above. Likewise, a review of periodical-literature would have doubled its size. The omission is regrettable but can be defended since the most important and central articles are often ultimately published in book-form and a number of these collections are reviewed below. Moreover, I have included, in Appendix B, a guide to the journals which the student of nineteenth-century British history is most likely to encounter and to find useful, with comments on their editorial policy, frequency and listing of bibliographical work, and general advice on their particular value as a medium of study. The output of periodicals is, indeed, intimidating and not even the most zealous teacher, let alone student, is ever likely to consult more than a selection of this specialised body of literature.

Mention might also be made here of other types of material that have not found a place in the body of this bibliography. Theses are sometimes useful to the student but are generally inaccessible, and again the best are, normally, eventually published. There is, however, a checklist in S. P. Bell, *Dissertations on British history, 1815–1914. An index to British and American theses* (1974), and the information presented there can be updated by reference to such publications as *Dissertation abstracts* and the annual supplement 'Theses completed' of the *Bulletin of the Institute of Historical Research*. Taped material is, as yet, on the evidence of that which is available, unlikely to usurp the place of the printed word. The Sussex Tapes are an enterprising attempt at bringing a couple of eminent historians together to debate before the microphone a central theme in history, such as Chartism, the industrial revolution, or the origins of the first world war. They do bring to the listener's attention some of the main areas of controversy, but personally I find the debates rather too polite, lacking in sufficient blood and thunder to reflect the cut-and-thrust of published historical debate. The Open University's radio broadcasts and some of the film material put together for television in Britain and increasingly in North America are much more useful. Some of this material can be obtained on loan or bought from the university, and the annual broadcast calendar gives the details of particular programmes and the times of their transmission. In this context it is worth mentioning the course-units which accompany these broadcasts, though they are far too numerous to review here. The reader of this bibliography will be especially interested in the units of the A401 course which cover such themes in nineteenth-century British history as elites, popular politics, and poverty and social policy.

The prototype of this bibliography was an article which I contributed to *Victorian Studies*, March 1976, in which I reviewed the materials available for teaching and studying the history of Victorian England. I am extremely grateful to that journal and especially to its editor, Martha Vicinus, for allowing me to make use of it here. This book, does in fact, depart in several major ways from the article. It covers a wider period. It is longer, surveys far more books and offers fuller comments. It includes sections which found no place in the article—such as that on Wales, Scotland and Ireland. It is arranged, by numbering each item, in a way which makes it a more handy source of reference. And it is, of course, more up-to-date, considering, as far as it was humanly possible, everything which seemed likely to merit inclusion down to the end of 1976 as well as some books published as late as the summer of 1977 immediately prior to the completion of my manuscript. The latter was possible because of the generosity of a number of publishers who kindly sent me their catalogues and review-copies. They are: Batsford, David & Charles, Longman Group, Macmillan Press, Oxford University Press, Penguin Books, Routledge & Kegan Paul, and Weidenfeld & Nicolson. I would also like to thank Martha Vicinus for sending me early in 1977 an advance-copy of the *Victorian Studies* annual bibliography for 1976; the librarians of Manchester Polytechnic and the Central Reference Library of Manchester for searching out many books which I have included here and many more which were omitted; and several of my colleagues for their valuable comments on parts of my manuscript—in particular, Terry Wyke (Sections 4–7), Mike Beames (Section 8), Brian Maidment (Section 9), and John Mosley for reading the whole. Any errors that remain are my own.

Finally, my deepest thanks are reserved for my wife. On one occasion, after a particularly arduous evening in the House, Disraeli, returning home to a pie and champagne supper, paid his wife the famous backhanded compliment—'You're more like a mistress than a wife'—presumably because the last thing she did was to talk politics. I owe Carol a similar debt of gratitude for allowing me the same respite from history.

DAVID NICHOLLS
October 1977

In the period between the completion of my manuscript and its setting in type I was able to review a number of books published in late 1977, and my comments on these are included in Appendix A.

D.N.
December 1977

1
GENERAL

The enormous output of specialist historical writings on nineteenth-century Britain produced in the last twenty years has meant that an up-to-date general survey embodying the conclusions of that research has become necessary and, in some respects, more difficult to write. Historians have, first of all, sought to right the imbalance created by the early and inveterate regard for high politics which characterised most historiography down to the 1950s. The result has been the production of some excellent general studies of economic and social history [see below, Sections 4 and 5]. We have, however, reached a point where the new knowledge and awareness needs integrating with the old—to move, as E. J. Hobsbawm has observed, from social history towards a history of society [see his essay in 505]. In other words, the future general historian must attempt to present a composite view of society which embraces the life of the humblest cottage-dweller as well as the machinations of the political elite. He will have a wide range of expertise to assist him—the skills of the economist, sociologist, demographer, political scientist, and so on. But as yet the conceptual analysis of the social scientist has been applied only in small part to writing on the nineteenth century.

The books in this section are considered in the following order: those covering all or most of the period 1815–1914; those covering the first half of the period; those covering the second half; and those covering short spans of about a decade.

1. R. K. Webb, *Modern England from the eighteenth century to the present* (1969)

A useful starting point for the undergraduate. It is a reasonable survey and fair summary of published material at the time of writing, though the reader with some knowledge of the period may find it rather tedious.

2. A. Wood, *Nineteenth-century Britain, 1815–1914* (1960)

Since its publication this has been a standard school textbook—and with much justification for, despite an emphasis on political history, it is a judicious survey. However, recent research has rendered it somewhat out-of-date, and a revised edition would not be unwelcome.

3. E. Halévy, *A history of the English people in the nineteenth century* (1913–46; 2nd ed., 6 vols., 1949–60)

A fundamental survey despite its age and size. The first volume, *England in 1815*, must still be counted among the best accounts of the country at the end of the Napoleonic Wars. Halévy did not, unfortunately, complete his mammoth undertaking, and the gap that he left (covering the years 1852–95) was filled less satisfactorily and with greater brevity by R. B. McCallum.

4. D. F. Macdonald, *The age of transition: Britain in the nineteenth and twentieth centuries* (1967)

A thematic account which, while it provides a fair overview of the period, does not, because of its tendency towards description, fulfil the promise of its title and provide an analysis of the nature of the transition.

5. D. Thomson, *England in the nineteenth century, 1815–1914* (1950)

A volume in the Pelican History of England series which provides a nicely structured, moderately priced, brief but dated introduction.

6. K. B. Smellie, *Great Britain since 1688: a modern history* (1962)

7. W. L. Arnstein, *Britain yesterday and today. 1830 to the present* (1966)

The sections on the nineteenth century in both of these are relatively short syntheses of modern research. Each is a volume in a wider series geared, apparently, to the general American market.

8. G. M. Trevelyan, *British history in the nineteenth century and after, 1782–1919* (1922; 2nd ed., 1937)

Now out-of-date, but a classic piece of Whig history which was, until recently, available in a cheap paperback edition.

9. L. C. B. Seaman, *Victorian England. Aspects of English and imperial history 1837–1901* (1973)

Surprisingly enough, the only one-volume general survey to cover precisely the Victorian era. As indicated by the book's subtitle it is somewhat selective in approach, but while not ignoring the major social, political and economic developments of the period, it does concentrate on certain areas which have often been neglected. For example, the 1890s, particularly the literature of that decade, is discussed at some length. On the whole, it is a thought-provoking introduction.

10. G. S. R. Kitson Clark, *An expanding society: Britain 1830–1900* (1967)
A collection of lectures which summarise the conclusions of recent scholarship on the responses of Victorian society to the forces unleashed by industrialisation.

11. N. H. Brasher, *Arguments in history: Britain in the nineteenth century* (1968)
An attempt to present polar arguments on particular controversial topics—whether the Whigs of the 1830s were reformers or reactionaries; whether Peel was a martyr or a renegade; if one can speak of a Victorian age, and so on. Some of the topics are not as controversial as Brasher imagines, and one occasionally feels that he is setting up Aunt Sallies in one section simply to knock them down in the next. But the debates do form a basis for seminar discussion.

12. E. L. Woodward, *The age of reform 1815–70* (1938; 2nd ed., 1962)

13. R. C. K. Ensor, *England, 1870–1914* (1936)
Two volumes in the Oxford History of England. They are both conventionally structured, particularly orientated towards high politics and largely superseded by more recent studies. Ensor is the better of the two and more likely to prove useful in the absence of a good survey of the late nineteenth century.

14. A. Aspinall and E. A. Smith (eds.), *English historical documents, vol. XI: 1783–1832* (1959)

15. G. M. Young and W. D. Handcock (eds.), *English historical documents, vol. XII (i): 1833–74* (1957)

16. *English historical documents 1815–70* (1964)
Rather old-fashioned and conventional collections drawn principally from official sources but nonetheless valuable within those limitations. The size of **14** and **15** makes them quite obviously library reference texts but **16** is a short selection from them.

17. G. M. Young (ed.), *Early Victorian England, 1830–65* (2 vols., 1934)

18. G. M. Young, *Victorian England: portrait of an age* (1936; 2nd ed., 1953)
The first, a collection of essays by seventeen writers, is uneven in quality but its most lasting piece, the brilliant 'portrait', was rightly

reprinted on its own. Its sparkling prose and penetrating insights provided the necessary antidote to the caustic studies of Lytton Strachey, and ensured for it a permanent place in any list of essential reading on the Victorian age.

19. A. Briggs, *The age of improvement, 1783–1867* (1959)

The best general introduction to the early nineteenth century. By meshing social with political and economic developments, and giving due place to the provinces as well as London, Briggs began the break with the sterile compartmentalisation and political orientation of more traditional history.

20. D. Beales, *From Castlereagh to Gladstone, 1815–85* (1969)

21. J. W. Derry, *Reaction and reform: England in the early nineteenth century, 1793–1868* (1963)

22. D. Marshall, *Industrial England, 1776–1851* (1973)

Paler 'age of improvement' studies which are generally well-written but are briefer and somewhat less stimulating than Briggs [**19**].

23. H. Ausubel, *The late Victorians. A short history* (1955)

24. T. L. Jarman, *Democracy and world conflict, 1868–1962* (1963)

25. T. A. Neal, *Democracy and responsibility: British history, 1880–1965* (1969)

26. H. Pelling, *Modern Britain 1885–1955* (1960)

Lightweight studies of the latter part of our period. **23** is a two-dimensional portrait of Britain in the hard times of the 'great depression' with documentary back-up material; **24** and **25** are factual accounts more suitable for school rather than college level; and the short narrative of **26** is neither well-structured nor satisfactorily integrated, though it is, as one would expect from this author, strongest on labour history.

27. R. Shannon, *The crisis of imperialism, 1865–1915* (1974)

A most disappointing attempt at filling a yawning gap in the general historiography of nineteenth-century Britain. Although it brings together the conclusions of much recent research, it is surprisingly old-fashioned history, strongest on politics and foreign policy, but wrongheaded on social structure, and almost entirely negligent of working-class movements. Its title is also misleading. However, it will no doubt hold the field until a better study emerges.

General

28. G. B. A. M. Finlayson, *England in the eighteen-thirties. Decade of reform* (1969)

29. A. Llewellyn, *The decade of reform: English politics and opinion in the 1830s* (1972)

These are two competent surveys, providing solid introductions for the student rather than offering any startlingly original insights.

30. J. W. Dodds, *The age of paradox. A biography of England, 1841–51* (1953)

A year-by-year account written in a rather literary style. This type of chronological narrative, imitating a biographical structure, is unusual and a little antiquarian for a general history, but there are some excellent illustrations and early photographs, and the book is a quarry of interesting information.

31. N. Gash (ed.), *The age of Peel* (1968)

A short selection of documents, a model of its type in that each document is placed in context.

32. W. L. Burn, *The age of equipoise: a study of the mid-Victorian generation* (1964)

33. G. S. R. Kitson Clark, *The making of Victorian England* (1962)

Two entirely different though equally excellent studies of the mid-Victorian years. 32 is an idosyncratic but delightful portrait which will give greatest pleasure to those who already have some acquaintance with the period 1850–67. It is particularly good on the family, and several aspects of social values and attitudes. 33 is a collection of lectures which called for a reassessment of mid-Victorian England. In drawing attention to those forces which shaped the period, it is strongest on political and social themes but rather weaker and lacking originality in its chapters on economic and demographic changes. It suggested important questions for future research.

34. H. M. Lynd, *England in the eighteen-eighties. Toward a social basis for freedom* (1945; repr. 1968)

Written a generation ago, this account of the challenge of collectivism in the 1880s and the inadequate response by government to it is deficient in many respects. But its lucid style and intelligent structure amply justified the accolade of the 1968 reprint, while it makes up a little for the absence of a good modern general survey of the later period.

35. D. Read, *Edwardian England 1901–15: society and politics* (1972)

36. D. Read, *Documents from Edwardian England 1901–15* (1973)

The most recent general survey of the Edwardian period, it lacks the colour of **38** and the originality of **494** but it is the best introduction incorporating the conclusions of modern research. The arrangement of the documents in the companion volume parallels that of the main text, a factor which partly compensates for the inadequacy of the comments on them.

37. S. H. Nowell-Smith (ed.), *Edwardian England, 1901–14* (1964)

A collection of essays with no single thesis which range in quality from the excellent chapters on 'Domestic life', 'Country childhood', 'The political scene', and 'The economy', through the more mundane accounts of 'The royal navy' and 'The army', to the positively uninspired three on 'Science', 'Thought', and 'Reading'. Major omissions are foreign policy and education.

38. G. Dangerfield, *The strange death of liberal England* (1935; 2nd ed., 1966)

This classic account of a moribund society has occasioned much debate and writing on Edwardian England. Even its severest critics who dispute its conclusions and dislike its impressionistic style would not deny that it is a 'good read'.

39. W. S. Adams, *Edwardian heritage. A study in British history 1901–06* (1949)

An interesting book which is little used, probably because of its thinly-disguised and provocative left-wing approach.

2
POLITICAL AND CONSTITUTIONAL

The number of studies in the field of political history and biography, for a long time the staple diet of historians, is so enormous that selection has had to be rigorous. For example, it has not been possible to include, in the realm of political theory, the numerous studies of Bentham, Carlyle, Kingsley, or James Mill, or the selections from their works which are slowly appearing. Nor, in terms of administrative history could space be found for the many monographs on government departments. While mainstream studies of political parties have been included, specialised accounts of the early origins of British Communism or of guild socialism have not. And the attempts which have been made to study the interplay of political ideas between Britain and America—notably to assess the impact of American democracy upon British politics—have similarly had to be excluded. The Victorian fetish for the large, often multi-volume, biography has meant that most of the age's great names are immortalised in print. Many were written by relatives or friends and are hagiographical. Their principal value for the present-day reader lies in their recourse to prolific quotation from private papers (though even here they are not always reliable). Most of them have been succeeded by critical and succinct modern studies and can be traced, if required, through the bibliographies of those studies. Some politicians still await a modern revaluation and for the time being the old biographies will have to suffice—for example, those of Forster, Harcourt, Ripon, Hartington, Hicks-Beach, Northcote, Aberdeen, Childers and Granville.

Despite this superabundance of political history there are still one or two surprising gaps. There is, for example, no history of the Liberal Unionist party. There is little on the early years of the Independent Labour party. And an up-to-date study of the nineteenth-century House of Lords would not be unwelcome. But, all-in-all, the student with the most voracious appetite for political history will have little difficulty in sating it.

For Irish political activity at Westminster, see Section 8.

General

40. W. Bagehot, *The English constitution* (1867; rev. ed. 1872; numerous reprints)

41. D. L. Keir, *A constitutional history of modern Britain since 1485* (1938; 9th ed., 1969)

42. H. J. Hanham (ed.), *The nineteenth-century constitution, 1815–1914: documents and commentary* (1969)

Bagehot's classic remains the finest account of the constitution at the time of the second Reform Act. **41** is the best textbook while **42**'s excellent commentary on a selection of key documents provides an invaluable introduction for the student.

43. A. L. Lowell, *The government of England* (2 vols., 1908; 2nd ed., 1912)

44. K. B. Smellie, *A hundred years of English government* (1937; 2nd ed., 1950)

For student purposes Smellie's account of the development of English government since 1832 is the best introduction to the political history of the period, but Lowell's detailed description and analysis is still worth quarrying.

45. C. Cook and B. Keith, *British historical facts 1830–1900* (1975)

46. D. E. Butler and J. Freeman, *British political facts 1900–60* (1963; 3rd ed., 1969)

45 would also have been more happily entitled British *political* facts. It contains several strange errors—such as the inclusion in a list of biographical notes on prime ministers, foreign secretaries and chancellors of the exchequer of the names of Bright, Cardwell, Chamberlain, Devonshire, Forster, Graham, Morley and Smith, the very details on which indicate that they never held such posts! Like its complementary volume on the later period, it will make a useful library reference text, but its prohibitive price will restrict it to that use.

47. E. C. Black (ed.), *British politics in the nineteenth century, selected documents* (1969)

This and its companion volume [513] provide a wide and fair selection of documents on nineteenth-century British history. The general introduction is a little over-simplified, but this is partly compensated for by a fuller introduction to each section, and a good guide to further reading.

48. K. Marx and F. Engels, *On Britain* (1954; 2nd ed., 1962)
Contains Engels's *The condition of the working class in England* [see also, **560**], as well as articles and letters by Marx and Engels on various aspects of contemporary British politics.

49. W. L. Guttsman, *The British political elite, 1832–1935* (1963)

50. W. L. Guttsman (ed.), *The English ruling class* (1969)
49 is important for its description of the political emergence of the middle class and for its analysis of the resilience of the old landed aristocracy. **50** is a collection of supportive documents.

51. F. E. Huggett (ed.), *What they've said about . . . nineteenth-century reformers* (1971)

52. F. E. Huggett (ed.), *What they've said about . . . nineteenth-century statesmen* (1972)
Selections of relatively familiar contemporary source-material and of later assessments by historians. The extracts are in general too short to be of much use, and the statesmen and reformers chosen are the expected ones.

53. R. Robson (ed.), *Ideas and institutions of Victorian Britain: essays in honour of George Kitson Clark* (1967)
Includes three essays on the realities of political power—D. Beales on the independent M.P. in the first half of the century; D. C. Moore on conventional impressions about 1832 and 1867; and J. Cornford on the 'Hotel Cecil', the political influence of Salisbury and his family. The essays are rather specialised but, of the remaining eight, four might profitably be consulted by students. They are: N. McCord on Cobden and Bright; H. J. Hanham on Scottish nationalism; O. MacDonagh on coal-mining regulations 1842–52; and G. Best on anti-Catholicism in mid-Victorian Britain.

54. G. Wootton, *Pressure groups in Britain 1720–1970. An essay in interpretation with original documents* (1975)
The best introduction to its subject, both as a history of private groups and also as a contribution to the debate on political modernisation. It contains abundant documentary material.

55. P. Hollis (ed.), *Pressure from without in early Victorian England* (1974)

56. N. McCord, *The Anti-Corn Law League 1838–46* (1958)
The period between the first and second Reform Acts was one of intense extra-parliamentary agitation, partly because the first of these

acts had been passed in response to such pressure, but also because of the activities of the most significant pressure-group of these years whose history has been comprehensively narrated in **56**. [See also, Chaloner's essay in **587**.] **55** is a collection of eleven generally well-executed essays which look at some of the less prominent pressure-groups (anti-slavery, suffrage, land reform, Liberation Society, Administrative Reform Association) and agitators (the Philosophic Radicals, Lovett, Shaftesbury, Edward Baines, David Urquhart). [See also, **453**.]

57. R. J. White, *Waterloo to Peterloo* (1957)

58. R. J. White, *From Peterloo to the Crystal Palace* (1972)

White considers the impact of popular politics on a system of government suited to the world of the eighteenth rather than the nineteenth century and sees the Peterloo massacre as a major turning-point after which violence gave way to parliamentary reform. The analysis in the earlier volume is less diffuse and more convincing than that of its successor.

59. J. E. Cookson, *Lord Liverpool's administration: the crucial years, 1815-22* (1975)

60. W. R. Brock, *Lord Liverpool and liberal Toryism, 1820-27* (1941; 2nd ed., 1967)

There is no satisfactory biography of Lord Liverpool or a good single-volume study of his years as prime minister, and together, therefore, these two accounts serve a dual purpose. **60** is particularly useful for its brief account of Liverpool's career before 1820; while **59** provides a stimulating thesis concerning the changing role of public opinion in the period under consideration, though its use of terminology (such as 'middling opinion', 'better sort' and so on) is unfortunately slack.

61. G. I. T. Machin, *The Catholic question in English politics, 1820-30* (1964)

A straightforward narrative of the campaign which culminated in Catholic emancipation. It sheds important light on party politics in the 1820s.

62. N. Gash, *Reaction and reconstruction in English politics 1832-52* (1965)

A collection of lectures by an authority on the politics of the period following the Great Reform Act, including two particularly succinct studies of the parties.

Political and Constitutional

63. T. L. Crosby, *Sir Robert Peel's administration 1841–46* (1976)
Contains little new material and hardly justifies the re-telling of a largely familiar story.

64. R. Stewart, *The politics of protection. Lord Derby and the Protectionist party, 1841–52* (1971)
The weak introductory chapters on the period before the repeal of the corn laws mar an otherwise excellent analysis.

65. W. D. Jones and A. B. Erickson, *The Peelites, 1846–57* (1972)

66. J. B. Conacher, *The Peelites and the party system, 1846–52* (1972)

67. J. B. Conacher, *The Aberdeen coalition, 1852–55. A study in mid-nineteenth-century party politics* (1968)
Conacher's two volumes (of a projected three) provide a minute and scholarly analysis of the shifting groupings of the middle of the century. 65 is shorter and offers a contrasting interpretation of Peelite politics.

68. K. Martin, *The triumph of Lord Palmerston. A study of public opinion in England before the Crimean war* (1924; 2nd ed., 1963)

69. O. Anderson, *A Liberal state at war. English politics and economics during the Crimean war* (1967)
68 was in many respects a pioneering study, but it should be used cautiously and read alongside the more balanced assessment of 69 which is, as its sub-title suggests, particularly strong on both politics and economic and financial policy.

70. P. Adelman, *Gladstone, Disraeli and later Victorian politics* (1970)
A volume in Longman's 'Seminar studies' series (distributed in North America by the same publisher). The books in this series, aimed at the popular student market, provide brief introductions to particular topics, selections of documents, and guides to further reading. The subjects chosen are often not especially controversial and the texts seem more prone to errors than is normal so that the pamphlets become historical abstracts rather than indicators of current debate, and their value for class discussion (though not necessarily for class preparation) is accordingly reduced. Adelman's is, however, one of the best of the series.

71. R. Rhodes James, *The British revolution. British politics 1880–1939. Vol. 1: From Gladstone to Asquith 1880–1914* (1976)
A good example of the way in which the word 'revolution' is

misused. (Normally one suspects that the gremlins have interpolated the letter 'r' in front of the more appropriate word 'evolution'.) A well-written account of the political personalities of the period, but little more than that.

72. A. B. Cooke and J. Vincent, *The governing passion. Cabinet government and party politics in Britain 1885–86* (1974)

The book is divided into two parts: a minutely-detailed 'Diary' of political events from 1 January 1885 to 5 August 1886 which occupies two-thirds of the space and is preceded by a 'Commentary' designed to show, amongst other things, that political change is best understood in terms of the caprice or calculation of an elite rather than as a response to social pressure. The new orthodoxy [cf. **110** and **112**] is more irritatingly empirical than the old.

73. H. Ausubel, *In hard times: reformers among the late Victorians* (1960)

Plugging the theme of **23**, this time by concentrating on the reformers flung up by the so-called 'great depression'. The information on the reformers and their causes is useful, but that the background against which that information is cast is grossly oversimplified can be judged from the two premises on which it is based: 'The English of the late Victorian era were a democratic generation. . . . They were also a depression generation.' The one is mistaken, the other misleading.

Monarchy

74. C. Hibbert, *George IV* (2 vols., 1972–73; 1 vol. ed., 1976)

75. P. Ziegler, *King William IV* (1971)

76. E. Longford, *Victoria, R.I.* (1964)

77. C. Woodham-Smith, *Queen Victoria: her life and times, vol. 1: 1819–61* (1972)

78. P. Magnus, *King Edward the seventh* (1964)

79. H. G. Nicolson, *King George the fifth: his life and reign* (1952)

There has long been a popular interest in the personalities of the occupants of the British throne. Strange, perhaps, because they were, for the most part, a dull bunch. The British public even manage to find Edward VII's hedonism endearing (though the sexual side of it is curiously played down by Magnus who either showed undue deference to Edward's successors or poor judgement of public taste). This fascination has spawned a whole host of biographies, ranging greatly in quality from the panegyrics of Albert which appeared periodically after his death (no doubt to soft-soap his widow), to the thorough, and on the whole, judicious ones to which the list has been confined.

80. F. Hardie, *The political influence of the British monarchy, 1868–1952* (1970)

81. F. Hardie, *The political influence of Queen Victoria, 1861–1901* (1935; repr. 1963)

Academic interest in the nineteenth-century monarchy has been largely confined to its residual political influence. Much information can, of course, be gleaned from the biographies mentioned above, but Hardie has performed a valuable, though not entirely satisfactory, service by concentrating in his two monographs on this particular theme. It is regrettable that no one has yet pushed it back further to embrace the influence of George IV and William IV, and, indeed, the young Victoria.

Central Government and Administration

82. A. J. Taylor, *Laissez-faire and state intervention in nineteenth-century Britain* (1972)

A volume in Macmillan's 'Studies in economic and social history' series (most of which are distributed in North America by Humanities Press, Inc.). On the whole an excellent series, designed for undergraduate consumption. The books are comparatively cheap. They offer summaries of the current historical debate on controversial topics by historians distinguished in each particular field, and a guide to the literature on that debate. Taylor's is concerned with the extent to which the first half of the nineteenth century was characterised either by *laissez-faire* or by gradual progress towards collectivism.

83. G. Sutherland (ed.), *Studies in the growth of nineteenth-century government* (1972)

84. V. Cromwell, *Revolution or evolution: British government in the nineteenth century* (1977)

85. P. Stansky (ed.), *The Victorian revolution: government and society in Victoria's Britain* (1973)

Subsumed in the debate summarised in **82** is a further disagreement concerning the role of ideas (particularly Benthamite ideas) in, and the mechanics of, the transformation of nineteenth-century government. The terminology used to describe this particular debate is, somewhat inappropriately, 'the revolution in government'. The principal protagonists in the dispute are O. MacDonagh and H. Parris, and their arguments, which originally appeared as journal-articles, have been reprinted in **85** along with a number of essays less apposite in terms of the debate, but stimulating in their own right—for example, D. C. Moore's 'The corn laws and high farming', D. Roberts's 'Tory paternalism and social reform in early Victorian England', and J. Cornford's 'The transformation of Conservatism in the late nineteenth century'. **83** is a collection of ten essays which illustrate current ideas and progress in the study of nineteenth-century government growth, and **84** a collection of extracts from documents and the writings of historians on the debate compiled for students. [See also, Jenifer Hart's essay in **505**, and **638**.]

86. A. V. Dicey, *Lectures on the relation between law and public opinion in England during the nineteenth century* (1905; 2nd ed., 1914; repr. 1962)

For a long time the most influential study of the growth of state intervention, but its oversimplified generalisations must be qualified by the more sophisticated arguments thrown up by MacDonagh and Parris.

87. O. MacDonagh, *A pattern of government growth, 1800–60: the Passenger Acts and their enforcement* (1961)

88. H. Parris, *Government and the railways in nineteenth-century Britain* (1965)

These two ostensibly narrow studies of transport history were the basic pieces of research from which the two authors drew their alternative explanations of government growth.

89. L. Brown, *The Board of Trade and the free trade movement 1830–42* (1958)

As well as providing useful information on the free trade movement, it is a case-study of the relationship between ideas and the policies of one government department.

90. W. C. Lubenow, *The politics of government growth. Early Victorian attitudes toward state intervention, 1833–48* (1971)

From case-studies of poor relief, public health, railway expansion, and factory legislation, Lubenow concludes that government intervention was a piecemeal response to particular crises. A major contribution to the debate.

91. H. Parris, *Constitutional bureaucracy. The development of British central administration since the eighteenth century* (1969)

Primarily concerned with the growth of administration from 1780 to 1870 but including also comments on the civil service in more recent times. Chapter 9 is a concise and clear rebuttal of the MacDonagh thesis.

92. O. MacDonagh, *Early Victorian government, 1830–70* (1977)

A straightforward synthesis of largely established knowledge about state intervention in major areas of economic and social activity. (The chapter on mines, for example, is mainly based on his own contribution to **53**.) It is, as MacDonagh says, a general book aimed at 'the sober first- or second-year undergraduate', and avoids returning to the debate with Parris. As such it is an unobjectionable introduction.

93. E. W. Cohen, *The growth of the British civil service, 1780–1939* (1941; repr. 1965)

An outline history. A more up-to-date analysis looking at, for example, the political influence of the civil service, is much needed.

94. W. I. Jennings, *Cabinet government* (1936)

95. H. J. Laski, *The British cabinet: a study of its personnel, 1801–1924* (1928)

96. J. P. Mackintosh, *The British cabinet* (1962)

Although **96** is now the standard history of the cabinet from its origins to the 1960s, **94** contains a satisfactory historical outline while concentrating on its workings, and **95** is a Fabian tract which includes useful statistical information about the ministers who comprised it.

The Electoral System

(a) GENERAL

97. J. Cannon, *Parliamentary reform 1640–1832* (1973)

The best introduction to parliament before the Great Reform Act. It is more approachable than the old two-volume study of the unreformed house of commons by E. and A. G. Porritt, and more up-to-date than G. S. Veitch's account of the genesis of reform. Chapters 8–11 are concerned with the post-1815 period, chapter 11 in particular providing a good contribution to the historical debate on 1832. Cannon takes as one of his themes the provocative remark by

J. F. Stephen that it was impossible to cite 'any single great change ... not carried by force, that is to say, ultimately by the fear of a revolution'. [See also, D. Fraser's essay in **587**.]

98. N. Gash, *Politics in the age of Peel: a study in the technique of parliamentary representation, 1830–50* (1953)

99. H. J. Hanham, *Elections and party management: politics in the time of Disraeli and Gladstone* (1959)

100. C. Seymour, *Electoral reform in England and Wales: the development and operation of the parliamentary franchise, 1832–85* (1915; repr. 1970)

98 and **99** together provide an admirable survey and sound analysis of the structure of British politics between the first and third Reform Acts, but they do seem, especially the latter, to have been overrated when set alongside Seymour's masterly account of 1915.

101. D. C. Moore, *The politics of deference: a study of the mid-nineteenth century English political system* (1976)

Uses the poll-books to provide a detailed analysis of voting patterns and behaviour in the pre-ballot era and to develop further his thesis on the conservative nature of early nineteenth-century electoral reform which he has previously presented in part in a number of articles. [See, for example, his contributions to **53** and **85**.]

102. H. J. Morris, *Parliamentary franchise reform in England from 1885 to 1918* (1921)

Intended as a sequel to Seymour [**100**] but amateurish by comparison.

103. H. J. Hanham, *The reformed electoral system in Great Britain, 1832–1914* (1968)

104. D. G. Wright, *Democracy and reform 1815–85* (1970)

105. J. B. Conacher (ed.), *The emergence of British parliamentary democracy in the nineteenth century. The passing of the Reform Acts of 1832, 1867, and 1884–5* (1971)

Three short but good introductions to the nineteenth-century electoral system and the changes wrought to it. **103** is an excellent précis in the form of an Historical Association pamphlet; **104** is one of the 'Seminar studies' series with their happy balance between commentary and documents [see **70**]; and **105**, despite its rather grandiose title, is a prosaic collection of source-material concerning the Reform Acts and with the background briefly sketched in.

(b) THE REFORM ACTS

106. J. R. M. Butler, *The passing of the Great Reform Bill* (1914; repr. 1964)

107. M. Brock, *The Great Reform Act* (1973)

106 was for a long time the standard source of information on the politics of 1832, but it has now been superseded by the thoroughly-researched and well-argued study by Brock.

108. G. A. Cahill (ed.), *The Great Reform Bill of 1832: liberal or conservative?* (1969)

109. W. H. Maehl (ed.), *The Reform Bill of 1832: why not revolution?* (1967)

Two short collections of extracts of controversial assessments of 1832, designed for students and normally eagerly seized upon by them as alternatives to reading the full accounts.

110. M. Cowling, *Disraeli, Gladstone and revolution; the passing of the second Reform Bill* (1967)

111. F. B. Smith, *The making of the second Reform Bill* (1966)

111 is a straightforward account of the passing of the act and, more important, of the context in which it was framed. By contrast, **110** is concerned to show that the character of the reform was determined by the manoeuvrings of the political elite and owed nothing to the agitation in the country—an analysis which must be compared with the contrary interpretation in **174**.

112. A. Jones, *The politics of reform, 1884* (1972)

An account of the political machinations leading to reform—in the style of Cowling [**110**] though possibly even more fogbound by its close attention to day-to-day detail.

(c) ELECTORAL FINANCE

113. W. B. Gwyn, *Democracy and the cost of politics in Britain* (1962)

Brings out clearly the extent to which the cost of electing and maintaining a representative in parliament ensured that such a career remained largely the preserve of the wealthy.

114. C. O'Leary, *The elimination of corrupt practices in British elections 1868–1911* (1962)

More narrowly conceived than Gwyn [**113**], this is concerned mainly with the period between the second Reform Act and the

Corrupt Practices Act of 1883 when the increasing cost of elections finally forced parliament to outlaw corrupt electoral expenditure.

(d) WOMEN'S SUFFRAGE [see also, **606–18**]

115. R. Fulford, *Votes for women: the story of a struggle* (1957)

116. D. Morgan, *Suffragists and Liberals. The politics of woman suffrage in England* (1975)

117. C. Rover, *Women's suffrage and party politics in Britain, 1866–1914* (1967)

There is no fully satisfactory history of the campaign for women's suffrage. **115** is readable but factual and thin; **116**, which is concerned with the period 1906–18, is both critical and confusing in its application of terms such as suffragist to supporters of both the moderate National Union of Women's Suffrage Societies (to whom it is usually applied) and the militant Women's Social and Political Union (to whom it is not); and **117** is a rather flat narrative unredeemed by its assessments, particularly of militancy.

118. E. S. Pankhurst, *The suffragette movement. An intimate account of persons and ideals* (1931)

119. A. Rosen, *Rise up, women! The militant campaign of the Women's Social and Political Union* (1974)

119 is concerned with confirming Mrs Pankhurst's own claim in **118** that the W.S.P.U. was the main vehicle responsible for winning the vote—an assertion for which Rosen's evidence is insufficient substantiation.

(e) ELECTIONS

120. H. Pelling, *Social geography of British elections 1885–1910* (1967)

Since this pioneering exploration of late Victorian electoral politics, detailed monographs of the general elections of 1880, 1906 and 1910 have appeared along with the publication of important source-material such as the poll-books and the electoral facts assembled by Dod and by McCalmont. It is to be hoped that this data will be processed at some stage. For the moment it is possibly a little too refractory for student consumption.

(f) LOCAL POLITICS

121. D. Read, *The English provinces, c. 1760–1960: a study in influence* (1964)

A tentative attempt to explore the role of provincial society which, while it relies heavily on the standard histories for references to local aspects of social and political movements, suggests an area for further study, though one, because of the imprecise nature of the concept of 'the provinces', not easy to develop.

122. R. W. Davis, *Political change and continuity 1760–1885: a Buckinghamshire study* (1972)

123. T. J. Nossiter, *Influence, opinion and political idiom in reformed England. Case studies from the North-east, 1832–74* (1975)

124. R. J. Olney, *Lincolnshire politics 1832–85* (1975)

These historians have been less ambitious than Read, and by confining themselves to precise and detailed analyses of regional politics, have written three excellent local studies from which it is to be hoped, it may be possible at a later stage to reconstruct a new synthesis.

Parliament

125. W. I. Jennings, *Parliament* (1939; 2nd ed., 1951)

Like his study of the cabinet [94], this is concerned primarily with the workings of the parliamentary machinery, but it does include valuable historical background.

126. J. A. Thomas, *The house of commons, 1832–1901: a study of its economic and functional character* (1939)

127. J. A. Thomas, *The house of commons, 1906–11: an analysis of its economic and social character* (1958)

Most useful for the statistical tables showing the economic composition of the parties represented in the different parliaments of the period, from which one can draw conclusions about, for example, the changing relative position of the landed and industrial classes during the nineteenth century.

128. W. L. Arnstein, *The Bradlaugh case. A study in late Victorian opinion and politics* (1965)

An excellent study of an infamous and discreditable episode in parliamentary history.

129. A. S. Turberville, *The house of lords in the age of reform, 1784–1837, with an epilogue on aristocracy and the advent of democracy* (1958)

Turberville unfortunately died before completing his history of the upper chamber. The main story therefore stops short at the accession of Queen Victoria, but it is the standard account to that date.

130. E. Allyn, *Lords versus Commons. A century of conflict and compromise, 1830–1930* (1931)

131. R. Jenkins, *Mr Balfour's poodle. An account of the struggle between the house of lords and the government of Mr Asquith* (1954)

130 is the only monograph to chart the changing relations between Lords and Commons in the century after 1830, though the outline of the story is familiar enough. Its climax is the constitutional crisis of 1909–11, which is also the subject of the engaging but superficial account by Jenkins.

Political Parties

(a) GENERAL

132. M. Ostrogorski, *Democracy and the organisation of political parties* (trans. by F. Clark, 2 vols., 1902)
Still worth consulting for its castigation of caucus politics.

133. I. Bulmer-Thomas, *The growth of the British party system* (2 vols., 1965)

134. W. I. Jennings, *Party politics* (3 vols., 1960–62)
Two large general surveys both containing information on the nineteenth century. **133** is to be preferred to **134** which suffers from too many errors and omissions, and is essentially an analysis of modern party politics.

135. D. Beales, *The political parties of nineteenth-century Britain* (1974)

136. A. Beattie (ed.), *English party politics* (2 vols., 1970)

137. S. H. Beer, *Modern British politics. A study of parties and pressure groups* (1965; 2nd ed., 1969)
Three dissimilar but equally valuable studies for student purposes —**135** for its brief but reliable outline in the form of an Historical Association pamphlet; **136** for the source-material it contains; and **137** for the short and stimulating way it places the contemporary British political system in its historical context.

Political and Constitutional

138. A. Bullock and M. Shock (eds.), *The liberal tradition from Fox to Keynes* (1956)

139. S. Maccoby (ed.), *The English radical tradition, 1763–1914* (1952: 2nd ed., 1966)

140. H. Pelling (ed.), *The challenge of socialism* (1954; 2nd ed., 1968)

141. R. J. White (ed.), *The conservative tradition* (1950; 2nd ed., 1964)

Four volumes of extracts from the writings and speeches of politicians and political theorists in A. & C. Black's 'British political tradition' series (distributed in North America by various publishers). It is a reflection of the similarities of the major parties that Joseph Chamberlain figures in every collection but Pelling's. Sir William Harcourt would, of course, have been nearer the mark had he said, 'We are all *liberals* now'.

(b) CONSERVATISM

142. R. B. McDowell, *British Conservatism, 1832–1914* (1959)

143. R. Blake, *The Conservative party from Peel to Churchill* (1970)

144. D. Southgate (ed.), *The Conservative leadership, 1832–1932* (1974)

There is no satisfactory history of the Conservative party. **142** is good on ideas and opinions in the party, and the collection of lectures brought together in **143** provides an excellent short guide, but neither is an attempt at writing a fully-rounded history. **144** is basically a collection of portraits of the recognised leaders of the party by historians whose views can, for the most part, be found in fuller studies elsewhere—Gash on Wellington and Peel; J. T. Ward on Derby and Disraeli; Southgate on Salisbury and Baldwin; A. M. Gollin on Balfour; and J. H. Grainger on Bonar Law. [See also, Cornford's article in **85**.]

145. R. L. Hill, *Toryism and the people 1832–46* (1929)

An interesting study of the 'points of contact' between the Tory party and the working classes—the origins of the notion, later known as Tory democracy, that landed aristocrats and labouring people could form a natural alliance against industrialists and manufacturers. A book which perhaps merits reprinting.

146. E. J. Feuchtwanger, *Disraeli, democracy and the Tory party* (1968)

147. P. Smith, *Disraelian conservatism and social reform* (1967)

Two very good studies which take up the theme of **145** but which prick the bubble of Tory democracy by demonstrating the extent to which Disraeli pursued Peel's goal of an alliance between the landed and the middle classes.

148. R. A. Rempel, *Unionists divided. Arthur Balfour, Joseph Chamberlain and the Unionist Free Traders* (1972)

One of the best accounts of the political implications for the Balfour administration of the tariff reform campaign.

(c) LIBERALISM

149. R. B. McCallum, *The Liberal party from Earl Grey to Asquith* (1963)

The only recent general survey, but it is a thin narrative which does not advance beyond the earlier ones by W. L. Blease and H. H. Fyfe.

150. A. Mitchell, *The Whigs in opposition, 1815–30* (1967)

The early chapters provide a much-needed analysis of the structure of politics in this period, and in particular discuss the basis of Whig–Tory rivalry.

151. D. Southgate, *The passing of the Whigs, 1832–86* (1962)

A very full narrative which looks at the resilience as well as the demise of Whiggism and also focuses on the response of Whig governments to particular issues.

152. J. Vincent, *The formation of the Liberal party 1857–68* (1966; 2nd ed., 1976)

153. D. A. Hamer, *Liberal politics in the age of Gladstone and Rosebery* (1972)

154. M. Barker, *Gladstone and radicalism: the reconstruction of Liberal policy in Britain, 1885–94* (1975)

155. H. V. Emy, *Liberals, radicals, and social politics 1892–1914* (1973)

156. P. Stansky, *Ambitions and strategies. The struggle for the leadership of the Liberal party in the 1890s* (1964)

157. H. C. G. Matthew, *The Liberal imperialists. The ideas and politics of a post-Gladstonian elite* (1973)

The Liberal party has attracted a whole host of historians possibly motivated by an urge to solve the riddle of its demise. Together they provide a sympathetic but full picture of Victorian Liberalism. **152** is a major study of grass-roots Liberalism and the centripetal influence of Gladstone, while for the later period **153** emphasises the search for an 'umbrella' programme to unite the factions, though this theme is rather heavily laboured. **154** charts the recovery of the party after the crisis of 1886, and **155** is especially useful on radical influence within it. **156** provides a lucid description of the internecine rivalries of the 1890s which culminated in the emergence of Campbell-Bannerman as leader. Lastly, **157** is an excellent study of an influential group within the party, though rather specialised for early undergraduate use.

158. C. Cross, *The Liberals in power, 1905–14* (1963)

159. P. Rowland, *The last Liberal governments. Vol. i: The promised land, 1905–10* (1968); *Vol. ii: Unfinished business, 1911–14* (1972)

160. K. O. Morgan, *The age of Lloyd George. The Liberal party and British politics, 1890–1929* (1971)

161. P. F. Clarke, *Lancashire and the new Liberalism* (1971)

By contrast with the Victorian period, Edwardian Liberalism has been less well-served. **158** is a conventional and somewhat insipid outline, and **159** a prejudiced and derivative narrative of events. This deficiency is partly compensated for by Morgan's introductory comments on a well-chosen selection of documents, and above all by Clarke's brilliant analysis of one particular region which seeks to show that Liberalism was neither moribund (*pace* Dangerfield, **38**) nor being squeezed out by a realignment of politics on class-lines [*pace* Thompson, **197**]. In Lancashire at least, Clarke argues, Edwardian Liberalism was the party of progressive social reform with a solid social base.

(d) RADICALISM

162. J. W. Derry, *The radical tradition: Tom Paine to Lloyd George* (1967)

163. S. Maccoby, *English radicalism* (6 vols., 1935–61)

Historians of radicalism have been reluctant to define the word and thus to give some coherence to their inquiries. Derry is content to provide only a collection of potted biographies, while Maccoby discusses radicalism at such length and under so many guises that it becomes identified simply with any movement for reform.

164. E. Royle, *Radical politics 1790–1900: religion and unbelief* (1971)

165. E. Royle (ed.), *The infidel tradition from Paine to Bradlaugh* (1976)

Two studies which bring out the secular strand in nineteenth-century radicalism, the first a contribution to the 'Seminar studies' series [see **70**], the second a compilation of annotated documents with a commentary.

166. D. A. Hamer (ed.), *The radical programme [1885]. By Joseph Chamberlain and others* (1971)

The major statement of radical aims on the eve of the Home Rule debacle.

167. T. W. Heyck, *The dimensions of British radicalism: the case of Ireland, 1874–95* (1975)

Employing a computer to analyse his findings, Heyck uses the test-case of Ireland to demonstrate the general malaise among radicals of the Liberal party at a time when they should have been urging collectivist policies. Like many historians of the Home Rule crisis, he overestimates the severity of the loss of Chamberlain to the party. (A reading of **166** will show just how limited Chamberlain's programme actually was.)

168. A. J. A. Morris (ed.), *Edwardian radicalism 1900–14* (1974)

Short essays by fifteen historians some of the best of which are developed elsewhere—for example, Lee on the press [**427**], and Koss on nonconformity [**802**]. Another example of the use of the term radicalism as a catch-all.

(e) LABOUR [see also 'Trade unions and labour relations' in Section 4 and 'Urban society' in Section 5]

169. M. Beer, *A history of British socialism* (2 vols., 1919; new ed., 1940)

For long the standard account of British socialist thought from medieval communism to socialism on the eve of the second world war, though superseded in part by recent research and by the chapters on Britain in G. D. H. Cole's massive general history of socialist thought.

170. G. D. H. Cole, *British working-class politics 1832–1914* (1941)

Concerned with working-class attempts to gain representation in parliament, but it contains a number of errors and should therefore be used cautiously.

171. G. Tate and A. L. Morton, *The British labour movement 1770–1920* (1956)
A Marxist interpretation of the growth of working-class activity in Britain. In 1957 the Communist party published a 'Study guide' to this book which provides a skeleton outline of its contents.

172. D. Kynaston, *King Labour. The British working class 1850–1914* (1976)

173. F. E. Gillespie, *Labour and politics in England, 1850–67* (1927; repr., 1967)

174. R. Harrison, *Before the socialists: studies in labour and politics, 1861–81* (1965)
172 is a disappointing attempt at filling a gap (particularly for the years 1850–70) in labour history. It makes no claim to originality, and as an amalgam of the conclusions of modern research on such themes as ideas, class, religion, culture and so on it is serviceable. But it is still necessary to turn to **173** which, despite its age, is the best introduction to the period following the decline of Chartism, and to the stimulating essays in **174**. The latter treats, in a controversial and thought-provoking manner, working-class responses to the American civil war, the role of militancy in the reform politics of 1867, the election of 1868, republicanism and other aspects of the activities of the proletarian left in the years 1869–73, and Positivism.

175. M. Morris (ed.), *From Cobbett to the Chartists. Nineteenth century vol. i: 1815–48* (1948)

176. J. B. Jefferys (ed.), *Labour's formative years. Nineteenth century vol. ii: 1849–79* (1948)

177. E. J. Hobsbawm (ed.), *Labour's turning point, 1880–1900: extracts from contemporary sources* (1948; 2nd ed., 1974)
Very useful anthologies of documents in the series 'History in the making'.

178. J. Saville (ed.), *Democracy and the labour movement* (1954)

179. A. Briggs and J. Saville (eds.), *Essays in labour history in memory of G. D. H. Cole* (1960)

180. A. Briggs and J. Saville (eds.), *Essays in labour history, 1886–1923* (1971)
Collections of, on the whole, excellent though rather specialised essays. The most valuable for student purposes are, in **178**, Daphne

Simon's on the neglected master and servant laws, and E. J. Hobsbawm's on the labour aristocracy [which is also reprinted in **181**]; in **179**, Briggs on 'The language of class in early nineteenth-century England' [which is also reprinted in **505**], S. Pollard on cooperation, E. J. Hobsbawm on 'Custom, wages and work-load in nineteenth-century industry', E. P. Thompson's discussion of the early years of the Independent Labour party in 'Homage to Tom Maguire', and Saville on the background to Taff Vale [which is also reprinted in **505**]; and, in **180**, Fred Reid on Keir Hardie, and Henry Collins on the Marxism of the Social Democratic Federation.

181. E. J. Hobsbawm, *Labouring men. Studies in the history of labour* (1964)

182. H. Pelling, *Popular politics and society in late Victorian Britain* (1968)

It is fascinating to compare the left-wing and right-wing of labour historiography represented in these two collections of essays, especially where they directly clash, as in their disagreement over the concept of the labour aristocracy. There are a number of other themes common to both—for example, the political influence of religion, or the early history of the Labour party—and it is impossible to do justice in a short space to either, except to say that taken together they provide marvellous material for classroom debate.

183. H. Collins and C. Abramsky, *Karl Marx and the British labour movement: years of the First International* (1965)

184. S. Pierson, *Marxism and the origins of British socialism* (1973)

Both useful for proving a negative—that Marxism was not very influential in terms of the early British labour movement—but rather marginal to most undergraduate courses.

185. A. M. McBriar, *Fabian socialism and English politics, 1884–1918* (1962)

186. N. and J. Mackenzie, *The first Fabians* (1977)

187. W. Wolfe, *From radicalism to socialism. Men and ideas in the formation of Fabian socialist doctrines, 1881–89* (1975)

188. M. I. Cole, *The story of Fabian socialism* (1961)

189. A. Fremantle, *This little band of prophets. The story of the gentle Fabians* (1960)

The Fabians have attracted an attention far out of proportion to their influence on the formation of the Labour party—probably

Political and Constitutional

because of the dynamic intellects which the society embraced. Indeed, much of the historical writing has been concerned with personalities—and this is as true of the work of interested parties such as Fremantle, a niece of Beatrice Webb, and Margaret Cole, herself a Fabian and the author of a study of the Webbs, as of recent 'scholarly' accounts such as **186** and **187**. As a result and because of its consideration of Fabian economic and political theories, **185** remains the best survey.

190. H. Pelling, *The origins of the Labour party, 1880–1900* (1954; 2nd ed., 1966)

191. P. P. Poirier, *The advent of the Labour party* (1958)

Little to choose between these two solid analyses. **190** does, however, contain some interesting material on the Labour Church movement.

192. F. Bealey and H. Pelling, *Labour and politics 1900–06; a history of the Labour Representation Committee* (1958)

193. J. H. S. Reid, *The origins of the British Labour party* (1955)

192 continues the story of **190** and includes the details of two vital events in the early history of the Labour Representation Committee—the Taff Vale judgement and the MacDonald–Gladstone pact. **193** covers much the same ground as **190** and **191** but is included here because it contains the fullest account of the early history of the parliamentary party down to 1914.

194. C. F. Brand, *The British Labour party: a short history* (1965)

195. H. Pelling, *A short history of the Labour party* (1961; 3rd ed., 1968)

196. P. Adelman, *The rise of the Labour party, 1880–1945* (1972)

Outline histories with the barest of details on the years before 1914. **196** does, however, as one of the seminar series [see **70**], serve its purpose as an introduction to historical writing and source-material on the Labour party.

197. P. Thompson, *Socialists, Liberals and Labour: the struggle for London, 1885–1914* (1967)

198. R. Gregory, *The miners and British politics, 1906–14* (1968)

199. K. D. Brown, *Labour and unemployment 1900–14* (1971)

Three specialist monographs for use by undergraduates at a relatively advanced stage. **197** is a penetrating analysis of the reasons for the slow growth of Labour in London; **198** is an exhaustive study of an important group whose transfer of allegiance from the Liberals to the Labour party was crucial in its early history; and **199** is a rather more limited account of the pressure brought to bear on the established parties by the nascent Labour group on a single theme—unemployment. Brown has also edited a collection of essays in 'anti-labour history' which look, occasionally rather narrowly, at some of the responses to the rise of a labour movement.

Political Thought

200. J. E. Bowle, *Politics and opinion in the nineteenth century: an historical introduction* (1954)

201. C. Brinton, *English political thought in the nineteenth century* (1933; 2nd ed., 1949)

202. W. Harrison, *Conflict and compromise: history of British political thought, 1593–1900* (1965)

203. D. C. Somervell, *English thought in the nineteenth century* (1929)

The study of political theory is more often than not reserved for politics rather than history courses. One reason might be the absence of a good introduction to the subject for the average student. **200** is sound but not confined to Britain; **201** is essentially a collection of pen-portraits of nineteenth-century ideologues rather than an interpretative analysis; **202** is written in a style calculated to deter any further interest in the subject; and **203** is a gallop at breakneck speed through the prevailing ideas and their proponents.

204. G. Himmelfarb, *Victorian minds* (1968)

205. S. R. Letwin, *The pursuit of certainty: David Hume, Jeremy Bentham, J. S. Mill and Beatrice Webb* (1965)

206. G. Watson, *The English ideology. Studies in the language of Victorian politics* (1973)

This group of studies is far more stimulating though more restricted in scope than the last. **204** is a collection of essays of uneven quality which originally appeared in a number of different publications; **205** sees its four subjects as representative of English thought, an interesting but not unchallengeable thesis; and **206** is the best of the lot, and of the seven books mentioned so far in this section the one to be urged most strongly upon an undergraduate readership. It is a thought-provoking if somewhat impressionistic study of the political language of several major nineteenth-century ideologues.

207. M. Cowling, *Mill and Liberalism* (1963)

208. J. Hamburger, *Intellectuals in politics: J. S. Mill and the Philosophic Radicals* (1965)

209. J. Plamenatz, *The English Utilitarians* (1949; 2nd ed., 1958; repr., 1966)

207 is disappointing both on Mill and on Liberalism; **208** is a limited but useful study of the Philosophic Radicals as a parliamentary pressure-group; and **209** an excellent introduction to Utilitarian moral and political philosophy and especially to the ideas of Bentham, and the Mills, father and son. In some respects John Stuart Mill's own autobiography and some of his essays (on Bentham, Coleridge, Liberty) offer the best insight into his character and philosophy. [See also, **216** and **506.**]

210. C. Harvie, *The lights of Liberalism. University Liberals and the challenge of democracy 1860–86* (1976)

211. M. Richter, *The politics of conscience: T. H. Green and his age* (1964)

212. G. R. Searle, *The quest for national efficiency. A study in British politics and political thought, 1899–1914* (1971)

Three illuminating but specialised studies of the contribution of intellectuals to Liberal politics—the basis, with the books of the previous group, for a future synthesis.

Political Biography

(arranged in alphabetical order by subject after the general collections, **213–17**)

213. L. Stephen and S. Lee (eds.), *Dictionary of national biography* (63 vols., 1885–1901) + supplements 1901, 1912 + *Dictionary of national biography, 1912–21* (1927)

A quarry of information, though inevitably the entries vary in quality quite considerably. It should be used with the 'Corrections and additions . . . cumulated from the Bulletin of the Institute of Historical Research' (1966).

214. H. van Thal (ed.), *The prime ministers* (2 vols., 1974–75)

Essays on the prime ministers from Walpole to Heath, many of them summaries, by their authors, of full biographies.

215. A. Briggs, *Victorian people. A reassessment of persons and themes, 1851–67* (1954)

216. G. Costigan, *Makers of modern England: the force of individual genius in history* (1967)

217. A. J. P. Taylor, *Englishmen and others* (1956)

215 is an attempt to impart something of the flavour of the mid-Victorian period through an examination of several of its more prominent characters. The selection is obviously open to criticism—every historian would no doubt choose differently if asked to select nine such 'representative' figures—but the vignettes of J. A. Roebuck, Trollope, Bagehot, Smiles, Thomas Hughes, Robert Applegarth, Bright, Lowe, and Disraeli, are skilfully drawn. Less satisfactory is Costigan's attempt to demonstrate 'the force of individual genius in history' through a collection of summaries of the orthodox biographies, putting it firmly in the unfashionable 'great man' school of history. The geniuses are Bentham, J. S. Mill, Newman, Disraeli, Gladstone, Beatrice and Sidney Webb, Lloyd George and Churchill. **217** contains amusing and idiosyncratic, one hesitates to use the word 'caricatures', 'portraits' is kinder, of Palmerston, Bright, Disraeli and Cobbett.

218. R. Jenkins, *Asquith* (1964)

219. S. Koss, *Asquith* (1976)

Both are well-written, the first a sympathetic, the second a rather more critical, assessment.

220. K. Young, *Arthur James Balfour: the happy life of the politician, prime minister, statesman, and philosopher, 1848–1930* (1963)

221. S. H. Zebel, *Balfour: a political biography* (1973)

222. A. M. Gollin, *Balfour's burden. Arthur Balfour and imperial preference* (1965)

223. D. Judd, *Balfour and the British empire: A study of imperial evolution 1874–1932* (1968)

There is no entirely satisfactory biography of Balfour. **220**, with its faintly bizarre sub-title, is a careful, though at times somewhat uncritical portrait, while **221** is superficial and unreliable. **222**'s account of Balfour's role in the tariff reform controversy is unconvincing. These deficiencies are partly compensated for by the thorough treatment of one aspect of Balfour's policy in **223**.

224. D. Tribe, *President Charles Bradlaugh, M.P.* (1971)
A detailed and disjointed study, clogged by its excessive regard for factual information. [See also, **128**.]

225. H. Ausubel, *John Bright: Victorian reformer* (1966)

226. G. M. Trevelyan, *The life of John Bright* (1913; 2nd ed., 1925)

227. J. L. Sturgis, *John Bright and the empire* (1969)
In the case of Bright, Trevelyan's uncritical but beautiful prose is to be preferred to the flat and uninspiring life by Ausubel or the stodgy thesis-turned book by Sturgis. [See also, **215** and **242**.]

228. J. Wilson, *C.B.: a life of Sir Henry Campbell-Bannerman* (1973)
There is nothing very startling in this biography of a genial though otherwise rather uninspired prime minister. But it is well-written and researched.

229. P. J. V. Rolo, *George Canning: three biographical studies* (1965)

230. W. Hinde, *George Canning* (1973)

231. P. Dixon, *Canning: politician and statesman* (1976)
Little to choose between these. They all contain the main ingredients and rely heavily on Temperley [**320**] for Canning's foreign policy. Hinde's more rounded portrait perhaps places her marginally ahead of the others.

232. C. J. Bartlett, *Castlereagh* (1966)

233. J. W. Derry, *Castlereagh* (1976)
The first is a well-constructed synthesis based on published sources, the second a pot-boiler produced, it seems, to fill a slot in a new series of political biographies rather than to say much that is new. [See also, **319**.]

234. J. L. Garvin, and J. Amery, *Life of Joseph Chamberlain* (6 vols., 1932–69)

235. E. E. Gulley, *Joseph Chamberlain and English social politics* (1926)

236. P. Fraser, *Joseph Chamberlain: radicalism and empire 1868–1914* (1966)

237. D. Judd, *Radical Joe. A life of Joseph Chamberlain* (1977)

238. H. Browne, *Joseph Chamberlain: radical and imperialist* (1974)

Despite the towering importance of Chamberlain in late nineteenth-century politics we have had to wait a long time for a biography that could be recommended to students. Now we have **237**, an excellent single-volume study. This has diminished our reliance on the friendly treatment of the massive six-volume official biography (**234**), the old but occasionally perceptive record of Chamberlain as social reformer (**235**), and the rather 'bitty' consideration of different aspects of his policies in **236**. **238** is one of the less satisfactory volumes in the 'Seminar studies' series [see **70**].

239. W. S. Churchill, *Lord Randolph Churchill* (2 vols., 1906; 1 vol. ed., 1952)

240. R. Rhodes James, *Lord Randolph Churchill* (1959)

Two fine studies of Randolph's political life, the later biography throwing some new light on his relations with Salisbury. Winston's study of his father's life is testimony to the fact that had he wished to retire from politics, he could have made a living as a historian. Both, sadly, turn a blind eye to the unsavoury aspects of Randolph's private life—understandable in a son, less excusable in a modern biographer.

241. A. Briggs, *William Cobbett* (1967)

There are several biographies of Cobbett, the fullest being that by G. D. H. Cole, the most balanced that by J. W. Osborne, and the most recent that by J. Sambrook. Briggs has, however, produced a short, useful account for students. [See also, **217**.]

242. D. Read, *Cobden and Bright: a Victorian political partnership* (1967)

There is no good modern life of Cobden. This comparison of the two radicals suffers by resorting to scoring points in Cobden's favour at Bright's expense, so that the latter's role is unnecessarily belittled. [Cf. McCord's essay in **53**.] Even the old life by John Morley was blighted by the jaundiced eye of a former disciple. There are also two narrow studies by J. A. Hobson and W. H. Dawson which throw light on Cobden's internationalist views and his foreign policy.

243. W. D. Jones, *Lord Derby and Victorian Conservatism* (1956)

A full study of Derby's life would be welcome—this neglects his private and social life and is thin on his early career. [But see **64**.]

244. R. Jenkins, *Sir Charles Dilke. A Victorian tragedy* (1958)

Too preoccupied with the sensational aspects of the divorce

scandal to provide the revaluation of Dilke's contribution to the Liberal party which is needed.

245. R. Blake, *Disraeli* (1966)

A masterpiece of style and, indeed, of compression when compared with the voluminous official biography. [See also **215, 216** and **217.**]

246. P. Magnus, *Gladstone: a biography* (1954)

247. E. Eyck, *Gladstone* (1938)

248. E. J. Feuchtwanger, *Gladstone* (1975)

249. J. L. Hammond and M. R. D. Foot, *Gladstone and Liberalism* (1952)

250. S. G. Checkland, *The Gladstones: a family biography, 1764–1851* (1971)

Historians are threatening to drown themselves in a sea of Gladstoniana. They are being borne down, to paraphrase the G.O.M., in a torrent of biographies, monographs, and published private papers. Since Morley's classic three-volume life appeared at the turn of the century we have had studies of Gladstone and Ireland [see **891**], of his foreign policy [see **322**], reminiscences by his son, and his private papers are now emerging from the rooms of Hawarden Castle more minutely, of his financial policies, his career at the Board of Trade, and his part in the Bulgarian agitation of 1876. His voluminous private papers are now emerging from the rooms of Hawarden Castle and the British Museum, where they have for so long been stored, and into the hard-covers resting on our library shelves. There, one can consult edited extracts from his diaries and autobiographical memoranda, as well as his correspondence with Lord Granville, and with the promise of more to follow. Despite all this no single study has yet appeared which does Gladstone full justice. **246** is a piece of resourceful compression, but possibly too resourceful. **247** and **248** are strong on Gladstone's political life, **249** on his peculiar brand of politics, and **250** an excellent account of his family and social background. But no single volume includes all these aspects—perhaps the task is an impossible one. [See also, **216**.]

251. W. D. Jones, *'Prosperity' Robinson. The life of Viscount Goderich, 1782–1859* (1967)

A valiant attempt to do justice to an otherwise forgettable prime minister.

252. T. Spinner, *George Joachim Goschen: the transformation of a Victorian Liberal* (1973)
Throws some light on the neglected topic of Liberal Unionism.

253. A. B. Erickson, *The public career of Sir James Graham* (1952)

254. J. T. Ward, *Sir James Graham* (1967)
Neither does much to alter the picture that emerged from Parker's official 'Life', but **254** is a succinct and more easily digestible modern study.

255. G. M. Trevelyan, *Lord Grey of the Reform Bill. The life of Charles, second Earl Grey* (1920; 2nd ed., 1929; repr., 1952)
The official biography which has not been surpassed.

256. K. Robbins, *Sir Edward Grey* (1971)
A craftsmanlike piece of modern scholarship.

257. E. Hughes, *Keir Hardie* (1956)

258. I. McLean, *Keir Hardie* (1975)

259. K. O. Morgan, *Keir Hardie: radical and socialist* (1975)
The two eminently readable biographies which appeared at much the same time are far superior to Hughes's polemic of over twenty years ago, though they are both stronger on Hardie's politics than on his personality.

260. F. M. Leventhal, *Respectable radical: George Howell and Victorian working-class politics* (1971)
Makes good use of a large manuscript collection to examine Howell's life as an example of 'the prevailing Liberalism of the politically conscious Labour aristocracy'.

261. C. Tsuzuki, *H. M. Hyndman and British socialism* (ed. by H. Pelling, 1961)
There is no satisfactory history of the Social Democratic Federation, and this study of the flamboyant personality who led it—a curious blend of aristocrat and Marxist socialist—is the best substitute.

262. R. J. Hind, *Henry Labouchere and the empire 1880–1905* (1972)
Labby's colourful personality deserves a modern life to replace the old account by Hesketh Pearson, but this doctoral analysis of just one aspect of his varied career is turgid.

263. C. A. Petrie, *Lord Liverpool and his times* (1954)
Liverpool still awaits a biographer.

Political and Constitutional

264. C. L. Mowat, *David Lloyd George* (1964)
265. J. Grigg, *The young Lloyd George* (1973)
266. W. R. P. George, *The making of Lloyd George* (1976)
267. K. O. Morgan, *Lloyd George* (1974)
268. P. Rowland, *Lloyd George* (1975)

The Lloyd George industry has enjoyed a recent boom, as these books (a small selection from the many that have appeared) testify. **264** is a short essay; **265**, a very promising start to a projected new biography; and **266**, making use of hitherto unpublished family papers, sheds new light on Lloyd George's early life; **267** is a brief life with plenty of pictures (following up an earlier short study by Morgan published in 1963); and **268** is the most recent, complete biography and probably the best to date, though, for the period of his life covered by this bibliography, **265** is to be preferred.

269. J. Winter, *Robert Lowe* (1976)

An excellent political biography of the albino Adullamite. His views on education have received separate treatment. [See also, **215**.]

270. D. Cecil, *The young Melbourne* (1939) and *Lord M.* (1954) (1 vol. ed., 1965)
271. P. Ziegler, *Melbourne* (1976)
272. D. Marshall, *Lord Melbourne* (1975)

Three good biographies but for different reasons. Ziegler seeks to correct the view canvassed by Cecil that Melbourne was uninterested in politics, and has produced a shrewd analysis of Melbourne's political ambitions to set alongside Cecil's entertaining account of his private and social life. **272** is a short synthesis, based largely on Cecil, written for a series of biographies of British prime ministers.

273. J. E. Wrench, *Alfred, Lord Milner: the man of no illusions, 1854–1925* (1958)
274. A. M. Gollin, *Proconsul in politics. A study of Lord Milner in opposition and in power, 1854–1905* (1964)
275. J. Marlowe, *Milner: apostle of empire* (1976)

The first is inexcusably bad—typified in his dating of the Bolshevik revolution as March 1917. The second is thoroughly researched and well-written but not a full biography. The third is solid but not very original and occasionally rather dull.

276. D. A. Hamer, *John Morley: Liberal intellectual in politics* (1968)
Elucidates one side of Morley's character, but this is not a portrait of its subject in the round.

277. E. P. Thompson, *William Morris: romantic to revolutionary* (1955; rev. ed., 1977)

278. P. Henderson, *William Morris: his life, work and friends* (1967)

279. P. Thompson, *The work of William Morris* (1967)
A many-sided individual like Morris, who could equally be included under political, or intellectual, or cultural history, is a bibliographer's nightmare! **277** is a first-rate study of Morris's socialism alongside which the other biographies pale in significance. **278** misguidedly tries to shatter the coherence and unity which E. P. Thompson has demonstrated lay behind Morris's many activities, an approach which is compounded by **279**'s separate and disjointed consideration of each of those activities. An excellent selection of Morris's writings has been edited by Asa Briggs. [See also, Redmond's essay in **506**.]

280. C. Driver, *Tory radical: the life of Richard Oastler* (1946)
An admirable study of a leading proponent of factory reform. It deserves reissuing in paperback.

281. D. Southgate, *'The most English minister . . .': the policies and politics of Palmerston* (1966)

282. J. Ridley, *Lord Palmerston* (1970)

283. D. Judd, *Palmerston* (1975)
These are the most recent of a fairly large number of attempts at rationalising Palmerston's sometimes erratic policies, but he still remains an enigma. **283** is a short, derivative study in the same series as **267** and **272**. [See also, **217**.]

284. N. Gash, *Mr Secretary Peel; the life of Sir Robert Peel to 1830* (1961), and *Sir Robert Peel; the life of Sir Robert Peel after 1830* (1972)

285. N. Gash, *Peel* (1976)

286. G. S. R. Kitson Clark, *Peel and the Conservative party: a study in party politics, 1832–41* (1929; 2nd ed., 1964)
The two volumes of **284** form a magisterial biography, indispensable to all students of the period. They have been condensed to a little

over a quarter of the original (285) for those lacking stamina. 286 is an old but instructive study. [See also, 63.]

287. R. Rhodes James, *Rosebery: a biography of Archibald Philip, fifth Earl of Rosebery* (1963)
A highly readable and well-paced biography.

288. J. Prest, *Lord John Russell* (1972)
A sympathetic and well-written study which tails off a little in considering Russell's later years.

289. G. Cecil, *Life of Robert, Marquess of Salisbury* (4 vols., 1921–32)

290. F. Kennedy, *Salisbury* (1953)

291. R. Taylor, *Lord Salisbury* (1975)

292. M. Pinto-Duschinsky (ed.), *The political thought of Lord Salisbury, 1854–68* (1967)

293. P. Smith (ed.), *Lord Salisbury on politics. A selection from his articles in the Quarterly Review, 1860–83* (1972)
A satisfactory single-volume life to replace Lady Gwendolen Cecil's uncompleted four-volume biography of her uncle has not yet appeared. 290 and 291 are merely pot-boilers, although the latter does, by concentrating on Salisbury's attitude to social reform, counterbalance the usual emphasis on his foreign policy [see, for example, 315 and 323–24]. Otherwise we have to make do with attempts to demonstrate from his various writings and speeches that Salisbury was at one and the same time a political empiricist (292) and an aristocrat neurotic about change (293). [See also, Cornford's essay in 53.]

294. J. L. and B. Hammond, *Lord Shaftesbury* (1923; repr. 1969)

295. G. F. A. Best, *Shaftesbury* (1964)
Although Best is in touch with recent research and makes use of material not available to the Hammonds, their assessment is still worth consulting. [See also, 55.]

296. C. A. Petrie, *Wellington: a reassessment* (1956)

297. E. Longford, *Wellington: pillar of state* (1972)
Petrie's 'reassessment' is totally unsatisfactory, while Longford's second volume of her life of Wellington (the first dealt with his military career) is better on his private than his political life.

298. B. Webb, *My apprenticeship* (1926), and *Our partnership* (ed. by B. Drake and M. I. Cole, 1948; repr. 1975)

A delightful autobiography based on her copious diaries. The first volume describes the childhood and early life of Beatrice Potter as she then was, the second her dynamic 'partnership' (through marriage) with Sidney Webb. [See also, **216**.]

Local Government
[see also, **121–24**]

299. S. J. and B. Webb, *English local government* (9 vols., 1906–29; repr. 1963 with 2 additional volumes)

Magisterial but imposing. The first four volumes are concerned with the history and operation of local government, the fifth with highways, the sixth with prisons, and volumes seven to nine with the Poor Law. The two additional volumes of the 1963 reprint are their *English Poor Law policy* and *The history of liquor licensing in England*.

300. K. B. Smellie, *A history of local government* (1946; 4th ed., 1968)

A masterpiece of compression when set alongside the Webbs' voluminous study, it is undoubtedly the best short guide to its subject, more approachable than the older accounts and sufficient for the general student on narrower topics such as the local government franchise examined more fully (in this case by B. Keith-Lucas) elsewhere.

301. W. Thornhill (ed.), *The growth and reform of English local government* (1971)

A collection of documents aimed at the student and the general reader. Thornhill provides a concise and lively historical introduction, and the documents are arranged in terms of themes (such as the structure of local government, London government, rates, exchequer grants, and so on) rather than chronology.

302. W. A. Robson, *The government and misgovernment of London* (1939; 2nd ed., 1948)

Approximately one-third of this book is concerned with the history of London government since 1835, and provides an informative introduction to the role of the City, the establishment of the metropolitan police force, and the setting-up of the London County Council.

303. E. P. Hennock, *Fit and proper persons: ideal and reality in nineteenth-century urban government* (1973)

Through a study of municipal government in Birmingham and Leeds, Hennock demonstrates clearly its increasing importance in the Victorian era [cf. **578**], a theme he had previously touched on in his contribution to **703**.

3
FOREIGN, IMPERIAL AND DEFENCE

Despite an amazing range and number of monographs on British foreign policy, particularly concerning Britain's relations with specific countries, there is still no general survey which one can confidently recommend to students. Most extant surveys, such as the three-volume *Cambridge history of British foreign policy*, have long been out-of-date. In fact, some of the best writing on British policy is included in the many books on international relations, consideration of which is outside the compass of this bibliography. A similar observation applies to imperial history. In this case, the numerous specialist studies are of Britain's role in the constituent parts of her empire, particularly in Africa and India, but it would be a separate task to produce a bibliography on the British empire. Nor is it feasible here, or for that matter particularly pertinent to most undergraduate courses, to include the many popular accounts of the campaigns, battles and leaders involved in preserving and extending that empire. The books I have omitted range from accounts of British infiltration of China to military operations against the Zulus; from the war in the Crimea to the making of the *entente cordiale*; and from the exploits in Africa of adventurers such as Rhodes and Mackinnon to the many biographies of diplomats long forgotten except by their historians. Generally, therefore, the bread has been thickly buttered, but there are still a few dry slices. For example, relations with Japan, curiously, seem to have received better treatment than Britain's relations with most of the European great powers and especially with Russia. The diplomatic side of Anglo-American affairs has on the whole been well charted, but its naval aspect rather neglected. And much military history is still being written by professional soldiers rather than professional historians.

Foreign Policy

(a) GENERAL

304. P. Hayes, *Modern British foreign policy. The nineteenth century, 1814–80* (1975)

Foreign, Imperial and Defence

The only recent general survey, it relies heavily on older studies and offers little that is new in the way of interpretation. Still, it must suffice as an introduction until a better one appears.

305. R. W. Seton-Watson, *Britain in Europe, 1789–1914, a survey of foreign policy* (1937)

The standard survey for forty years, it remains an admirable introduction to British foreign policy down to the Congress of Berlin, but is rather thin on developments after that event.

306. K. Bourne, *The foreign policy of Victorian England 1830–1902* (1970)

307. A. J. Marcham, *Foreign policy* (1973)

308. H. W. V. Temperley and L. M. Penson (eds.), *Foundations of British foreign policy from Pitt (1792) to Salisbury (1902); or documents, old and new, selected and edited, with historical introductions* (1938; repr. 1966)

309. J. B. Joll (ed.), *Britain and Europe: Pitt to Churchill, 1793–1940* (1950)

310. J. H. Wiener (ed.), *Great Britain: foreign policy and the span of empire, 1689–1971* (4 vols., 1972)

311. C. J. Lowe, *The reluctant imperialists: British foreign policy, 1878–1902* (2 vols., 1967)

312. C. J. Lowe and M. L. Dockrill, *The mirage of power: British foreign policy, 1902–22* (3 vols., 1972)

Despite their reluctance to write a general survey, modern historians have not been slow to produce collections of documents with commentaries, as this list well testifies. By careful dissection of these books the astute student can extract the bones of nineteenth-century British foreign policy. **306** is a good starting point. It contains a practical introduction, followed by a well-chosen selection of documents and an excellent bibliographical essay. **307** is one of Methuen's 'Examining the evidence' series, edited by L. W. and E. E. Cowie, the volumes of which are an attempt to link together a range of documentary material on a single theme by a fairly full text. But they fall rather awkwardly between the usual collection with a brief commentary, and the textbook replete with extensive quotations. Moreover, they rely almost exclusively on printed evidence, and therefore offer neither a full selection for the reader to come to his own conclusions nor a critical assessment of the conclusions drawn by historians who have examined all the evidence. For the rest, the sub-title of **308** says it all; **309** is a reasonable substitute for **306**; **310** is a lengthy companion to **514**; and the commentaries in **311** and **312** are valuable summations of current research.

(b) MONOGRAPHS

313. A. J. P. Taylor, *The troublemakers: dissent over foreign policy, 1792–1939* (1957)

314. A. J. A. Morris, *Radicalism against war 1906–14. The advocacy of peace and retrenchment* (1973)

The theme of Radical opposition to official foreign policy surveyed in the suggestive and stimulating lectures of **313** has not, generally, been taken up [though Radical criticism of imperial policy has—see **350–52**], apart from in **314**'s somewhat opaque study of the pre-war period.

315. C. H. D. Howard, *Splendid isolation: a study of ideas concerning Britain's international position and foreign policy during the later years of the Third Marquis of Salisbury* (1967)

316. C. H. D. Howard, *Britain and the 'casus belli', 1822–1902* (1974)

Two interpretative essays. The theme, spelt out lengthily in the title, but examined succinctly in the text, of the earlier book is projected back in **316** into an inquiry into the reasons for the reluctance of British governments generally in the nineteenth century to commit themselves to continental alliances and guarantees.

317. G. Monger, *The end of isolation: British foreign policy, 1900–07* (1963)

A significant era of British foreign policy solidly analysed. The importance of the book's theme is highlighted when read alongside **315** and **316**.

318. Z. S. Steiner, *The Foreign Office and foreign policy 1898–1914* (1969)

A major study of policy-making within the Foreign Office at a period in its peace-time history when it was probably least hampered by accountability to parliament.

(c) PRACTITIONERS [see also, 'Political Biography' in Section 2]

319. C. K. Webster, *The foreign policy of Castlereagh, 1815–22. Britain and the European alliance* (1925; 2nd ed., 1934; repr. 1958)

The second volume of a monumental study of Castlereagh's foreign policy (the first covers the years 1812–15), concerned primarily with his attempts to institute a new system of diplomacy during the period of the Congress system.

320. H. W. V. Temperley, *The foreign policy of Canning, 1822–27* (1925)

Still worth consulting, though gutted by Canning's later biographers.

321. C. K. Webster, *The foreign policy of Palmerston, 1830–41: Britain, the liberal movement, and the eastern question* (2 vols., 1951)

Scholarly account of the 'liberal abroad' though possibly too detailed for the student faced already with two very long biographies [**281** and **282**].

322. P. Knaplund, *Gladstone's foreign policy* (1935; repr. 1970)
Somewhat dated but still worth its reprint.

323. J. A. S. Grenville, *Lord Salisbury and foreign policy: the close of the nineteenth century* (1964)

324. C. J. Lowe, *Salisbury and the Mediterranean, 1886–96* (1965)
Two excellent monographs, the first of which in particular goes far towards compensating for the absence of a fully-rounded biography.

Imperialism

(a) THEORIES

325. A. G. L. Shaw (ed.), *Great Britain and the colonies, 1815–65* (1970)

326. M. E. Chamberlain, *The new imperialism* (1970)

327. R. W. Winks (ed.), *British imperialism: gold, God, glory* (1963)
The literature on theories of imperialism is far too vast to review here. Most of the general explanations of imperialism are concerned solely neither with the British experience nor with the nineteenth century. It is impossible, however, to understand nineteenth-century British expansion without some comprehension of the theoretical debate largely spurred by Lenin's critique in 1916 of imperialism as the highest stage of capitalist exploitation. The three books listed here provide introductions to that debate—the first by

reprinting important recent articles on a period once generally held to have been anti-imperialist; the second by summarising in a short Historical Association pamphlet the arguments about whether or not the late nineteenth century saw a new scramble for colonies; and the third by assembling extracts from the principal protagonists in the debate, from Lenin to Schumpeter. It is unfortunate that much of the controversy has been created by critics preoccupied with demolishing their own bowdlerised versions of what Lenin actually wrote. His analysis of 1916 was concerned not just with the rapid division of the world between the Great Powers in the period 1870–1900 but also with the *re-division* which, he argued, capitalist rivalries inevitably entailed once the original partition was completed and which had resulted in world war.

328. R. L. Schuyler, *The fall of the old colonial system. A study in British free trade 1770–1870* (1945)

329. B. Semmel, *The rise of free trade imperialism: classical political economy, the empire of free trade, and imperialism, 1750–1850* (1970)

330. D. C. M. Platt, *Finance, trade and politics: British foreign policy 1815–1914* (1968)

329 is essentially a refutation of the old view, presented in 328, which saw in the demise of mercantilism and the rise of free trade an anti-imperialist spirit. It takes up ideas originally put forward by Ronald Robinson and John Gallagher in an article entitled 'The imperialism of free trade' and which is reprinted in 325. 330 is an important response to these revisionist arguments and sees policy as being primarily determined by political rather than economic considerations.

(b) GENERAL

331. E. A. Benians (et al.), *Cambridge history of the British empire* (3 vols., 1929–59)

332. C. E. Carrington, *The British overseas. Exploits of a nation of shopkeepers* (1950; 2nd ed., 1968)

333. J. E. Bowle, *The imperial achievement. The rise and transformation of the British empire* (1974)

334. R. Hyam, *Britain's imperial century 1815–1914. A study of empire and expansion* (1976)

335. B. Porter, *The lion's share. A short history of British imperialism 1850–1970* (1976)

Until very recently there was no introductory survey of nineteenth-century imperialism which one could confidently recommend. There were, admittedly, several coffee-table picture books and a number of tub-thumping accounts by die-hard imperialists. There was also the heavily political and dated Cambridge history, its three volumes appearing before the intensification of the debate on theories of imperialism in the 1960s, and the valuable narrative of **332** which suffered from the same unavoidable difficulty. However, we now have a cheap and readily accessible paperback narrative (**333**) to replace Carrington; an authoritative account of nineteenth-century British imperialism in **334**, which in its two parts combines a general survey with a number of regional studies, though its suggestion that the Victorians' zest for empire can be understood in terms of their surplus sexual energy is intriguing rather than convincing; and, lastly, a summary in **335** of the debate and findings of the last twenty years which, despite its downplaying of economic explanations of imperialism, must now be counted the best introduction to its subject.

336. C. J. Bartlett (ed.), *Britain pre-eminent: studies in British world influence in the nineteenth century* (1969)

337. D. A. Low, *Lion rampant. Essays in the study of British imperialism* (1973)

338. R. Hyam and G. Martin, *Reappraisals in British imperial history* (1975)

Refreshing if not always convincing attempts to move the study of imperialism to new planes. **337** in particular reflects the growing interest among historians in questions concerning the nature of imperial authority, and the impact of imperialism on colonial societies and their differing responses to it. The collection of essays brought together in **336** seeks to get away from the debate about the aims of imperialists by looking at the spread of British technology, capital, and people to the world at large, not just the colonies. The idea was good but its execution somewhat disappointing. The difficulty of measuring 'influence' in quantifiable terms has not been satisfactorily confronted. But, like the other books mentioned here, it provides a new angle on its subject which will no doubt be explored further in the future. Two of the ten essays in **338** are particularly useful for general students—Martin's discussion of anti-imperialism in the mid-nineteenth century and Hyam's critique of Robinson and Gallagher's account of the partition of Africa [see **347**].

(c) MONOGRAPHS

339. W. P. Morrell, *British colonial policy in the age of Peel and Russell* (1930; repr. 1966)

340. W. P. Morrell, *British colonial policy in the mid-Victorian age: South Africa, New Zealand, the West Indies* (1969)

Two thoroughly researched and competent studies which, while they make no contribution as such to the debate on the imperialism of free trade, provide plenty of ammunition for its protagonists.

341. C. A. Bodelsen, *Studies in mid-Victorian imperialism* (1924; 2nd ed., 1960)

Detailed, and superseded in part by **340**.

342. C. C. Eldridge, *England's mission: the imperial idea in the age of Gladstone and Disraeli 1868–80* (1973)

A closely-argued study which considers whether or not there was a marked departure in British imperial policy in the 1870s.

343. J. Morris, *Pax Britannica: the climax of an empire* (1968)

344. M. Beloff, *Imperial sunset. Vol. 1: Britain's liberal empire, 1897–1921* (1969)

343 is an impressionistic but entertaining attempt to recapture the flavour of the British empire at its height, and **344** a stimulating analysis of its decline.

345. J. Hatch, *The history of Britain in Africa. From the fifteenth century to the present* (1969)

346. M. E. Chamberlain, *The scramble for Africa* (1974)

347. R. Robinson and J. Gallagher, with A. Denny, *Africa and the Victorians* (1961)

348. G. N. Uzoigwe, *Britain and the conquest of Africa: the age of Salisbury* (1974)

The partition of Africa has been both the inspiration and the testing-ground for the theories of imperialism. The hundred or so pages of **345** on the nineteenth century and the 'Seminar study' by Chamberlain [see **70**] provide good, short introductions to the debate on the partition. Robinson and Gallagher's thesis that British intervention was primarily a response to proto-nationalist rebellions in Africa itself which threatened the Suez route to India, is justly famous and the stimulus of much debate. **348** partly reflects the new trend in the historiography of empire by concentrating on African resistance to imperialism, and partly some of its old defects by its emphasis on Salisbury's role.

349. T. C. Caldwell (ed.), *The Anglo-Boer war. Why was it fought? Who was responsible?* (1965)

The literature on the Boer war, its antecedents (e.g. the Jameson Raid), and its aftermath (e.g. the Union) is now quite large, and this pamphlet with a selection from it and a guide to further reading is a useful starting-point.

350. A. P. Thornton, *The imperial idea and its enemies* (1959)

351. B. Semmel, *Imperialism and social reform: English social-imperial thought 1895–1914* (1960)

352. B. Porter, *Critics of empire: British Radical attitudes to colonialism in Africa, 1895–1914* (1968)

353. R. Price, *An imperial war and the British working class: working-class attitudes and reactions to the Boer war, 1899–1902* (1972)

Radical and left-wing reactions to the imperialist fervour of the late Victorian and Edwardian periods have been fully charted in the first three volumes listed here. By contrast, **353** analyses working-class responses to the Boer war and challenges, not entirely convincingly, the established view that they were jingoistic. [Cf. Pelling's essay on this subject, in **182**.]

Defence

(a) GENERAL

354. F. A. Johnson, *Defence by committee: the British Committee of Imperial Defence, 1885–1959* (1960)

355. N. d'Ombrain, *War machinery and high policy: defence administration in peacetime Britain, 1902–14* (1973)

356. S. R. Williamson Jr., *The politics of grand strategy: Britain and France prepare for war 1904–14* (1969)

Overall defence planning in the nineteenth century has attracted little attention, partly because it was virtually non-existent before the setbacks in the Boer war shook British complacency. Thereafter, and down to the first world war, the Committee of Imperial Defence came into its own, and d'Ombrain's account of its history in this crucial period is superior to Johnson's. **356** is a masterly account of the evolution of the Anglo-French *entente* from an amicable settlement of past disputes to an arrangement for future war, and the implications of this development for the crisis of 1914.

(b) THE ARMY

357. C. Barnett, *Britain and her army 1509–1970. A military, political and social survey* (1970)

Of the several popular histories of the British army, this illustrated account, because it surveys the political and social background, is marginally the best.

358. J. Luvaas, *The education of an army: British military thought, 1815–1940* (1965)

A consideration of the ideas of a number of writers of military theory rather than the more general and much-needed analysis implied in the title.

359. W. S. Hamer, *The British army: civil-military relations, 1885–1905* (1970)

Essentially a piece of administrative history, possibly too specialised in its account of the changing relations between soldiers and bureaucrats for early student use.

360. H. de Watteville, *The British soldier: his daily life from Tudor to modern times* (1954)

361. B. Mollo, *The British army from old photographs* (1975)

360 is one of a number of popular social histories of the army and gives some insight into a soldier's life in the last century, though the photographs of **361**, assembled from the collection in the National Army Museum, convey almost as much.

(c) THE NAVY

362. P. M. Kennedy, *The rise and fall of British naval mastery* (1976)

Covering the period from the Tudors to recent times and relating sea-power to Britain's economic strength, this is the best general history, superseding a large number of popular accounts.

363. C. J. Bartlett, *Great Britain and sea power, 1815–53* (1963)

364. G. S. Graham, *The politics of naval supremacy: studies in British maritime ascendancy* (1965)

Two sound though not particularly penetrating studies of naval superiority and the Pax Britannica.

365. A. J. Marder, *The anatomy of British sea power: a history of British naval policy in the pre-Dreadnought era, 1880–1905* (1940; repr. 1964)

366. A. J. Marder, *From the Dreadnought to Scapa Flow. Vol. i: The road to war, 1904–14* (1961)

367. E. L. Woodward, *Great Britain and the German navy* (1935; repr. 1964)

The two volumes by Marder are standard for all aspects of naval history in the latter part of our period, though Woodward's earlier account of the rivalry stimulated by Tirpitz's naval programme stands up well against them.

368. R. F. Mackay, *Fisher of Kilverstone* (1973)

The best biography—excellent also for the light it sheds on naval history during Fisher's lifetime.

369. P. Kemp, *The British sailor. A social history of the lower deck* (1970)

370. M. Lewis, *The navy in transition, 1814–64: a social history* (1965)

371. W. P. Trotter, *The royal navy in old photographs* (1975)

The two (of eleven) chapters of **369** on the nineteenth century provide a short survey of social conditions from pay to punishment. By contrast, **370** is a more detailed account of the gradual 'professionalisation' of the navy. **371** is less useful as a piece of social history than its companion volume on the army [**361**] but those who like looking at photographs of old ships will find it interesting.

372. D. M. Schurman, *The education of a navy: the development of British naval strategic thought, 1867–1914* (1965)

Tends to suffer from the same defect as Luvaas's study of military thought [**358**] in that it concentrates on the ideas of individual writers of naval theory. But it does bring out clearly the neglect of coherent strategic planning in the royal navy.

4
ECONOMIC

Economic history is now very much a discipline in its own right, most British universities and polytechnics have separate departments of economic history, and the subject has its own body of specialised literature. The books included here are but the tip of the iceberg. For example, nearly all the major and many of the minor industries have at least one monograph. They range from textiles, mining, iron and steel, engineering, and shipbuilding to chairmaking and pottery; from regional studies of industrial development to biographies of prominent industrialists. I have, however, included a study of coalmining which is short enough to serve as an example of this 'industrial' history; monographs on the cotton famine because of its social significance; histories of the press (though not of individual newspapers or the press barons) because of its social and cultural as well as economic importance; and transport studies which have developed in recent years into almost a separate field of historical inquiry. Even in the case of the latter, however, it is not possible to consider more than a sample of the enormous literature which now exists, and I have excluded books on specific branches of transport history other than the railways which had a tremendous impact on all aspects of Victorian life. But vintage-car enthusiasts can, if they wish, probably find a history of the development of their own particular favourite. Likewise, I have ignored specialised studies of farming techniques, banking, currency, taxation, insurance and other questions of finance, the retailing revolution, the development of public utilities (such as electric lighting, gas and water supply, and the fire service), the theories of the classical economists, and the growth of technology. These topics, and accounts of the major industries, are covered, however, at a level sufficient for the readership at which this bibliography is pitched, in most of the general books reviewed in the first part of this section. Most of the major trade-union histories have been included, but for others less important the student should turn to R. and E. Frow and M. Katanka, *The history of British trade unionism: a select bibliography*, an Historical Association pamphlet of 1969. For information on individuals within the trade-union and labour movement the four volumes so far published of the *Dictionary of labour biography*, edited by J. M. Bellamy and J. Saville, are invaluable, especially for the information they provide on local leaders, who rarely receive sufficient attention in the history books. I have also deliberately excluded histories specifically of the industrial revolution which are more appropriate to a bibliography on the eighteenth century.

The books that follow do, however, give a fair indication of the range of material available and one can use Chaloner and Richardson's bibliography [see p. 11] to track down the more detailed monographs as well as articles. Many of the books in the section on social history [see, for example, under 'Population' and 'Urban society' and 'Rural society'] and political history [56, for example, provides sufficient background on the corn laws, and the essay by Pollard in 179 a brief introduction to cooperation] are also relevant. Economic historians have in fact left very few stones to upturn. Some industries, such as fishing, and more seriously cotton, still require a good modern history. Differences in local farming techniques and, indeed, regional economic developments generally, are only just beginning to be studied. But, the research that remains to be done is in areas too narrow to be of direct interest to most history undergraduates.

General

373. S. Pollard and D. W. Crossley, *The wealth of Britain 1085–1966* (1968)

374. B. Murphy, *A history of the British economy 1086–1970* (1973)

Two very general surveys which are good starting points for those with little previous knowledge of nineteenth-century economic history, particularly as both contain guidance on further reading.

374 is also available in two parts which means less expense for those interested in buying only the modern history (1740–1970).

375. P. Gregg, *A social and economic history of Britain 1760–1970* (1950; 6th ed., 1971)

376. R. Tames, *Economy and society in nineteenth-century Britain* (1972)

377. M. W. Flinn, *An economic and social history of Britain since 1700* (1963; 2nd ed., 1975)

Three basic textbooks which cover social as well as economic history, and of a type very popular with students. They can, however, be relied on too exclusively to the extent that they become a substitute for more detailed reading. **376** in particular should be treated with great care.

378. C. R. Fay, *Great Britain from Adam Smith to the present day. An economic and social survey* (1928; 5th ed., 1950)

379. A. Redford, *The economic history of England [1760–1860]* (1931; 2nd ed., 1960)

380. J. H. Clapham, *An economic history of modern Britain* (3 vols., 1926–38)

381. W. H. B. Court, *A concise economic history of Britain, from 1750 to recent times* (1954)

382. W. W. Rostow, *The British economy of the nineteenth century* (1948)

A selection of the best of the older studies. All of them, though superseded to some extent by more recent research, are works of mature scholarship. **378** and **379**, excellent syntheses for their time, have been justly reprinted, the former several times. **380**, a monumental study which defined many of the questions which economic historians should pursue, is still approachable by students, at least in parts. **381** is an admirable piece of compressed history, though admittedly somewhat dull. And the framework established in **382**, though now generally rejected, is still worth consulting as the source of much subsequent debate and as an introduction to the ideas of a prominent theorist.

383. E. J. Hobsbawm, *Industry and empire. From 1750 to the present day* (1968)

384. P. Mathias, *The first industrial nation; an economic history of Britain 1700–1914* (1969)

As introductions to the nineteenth-century British economy these two books cannot be bettered. Hobsbawm has succeeded in writing an economic history for the general reader which interweaves economic and social change but is unencumbered by economic theory. Its chapters on the oft-neglected economic development of Scotland and Wales and its low price in paperback make it especially good value. **384** is straight economic history, surveying matters of production, distribution, and exchange; firmly grounded in abundant statistical evidence, it conveys a smooth, coherent picture of economic development from the advent of industrialisation to the first world war.

385. W. H. B. Court (ed.), *British economic history, 1860–1914: commentary and documents* (1965)

386. R. W. Breach and R. M. Hartwell (eds.), *British economy and society, 1870–1970: documents, descriptions, statistics* (1972)

387. B. W. Clapp (ed.), *Documents in English economic history. England since 1760* (1976)

Three collections of documents with commentaries which are particularly useful for introducing the student to the raw materials of economic history.

388. J. D. Chambers, *The workshop of the world: British economic history from 1820 to 1880* (1961)

389. S. G. Checkland, *The rise of industrial society in England 1815–85* (1964)

Two lucid guides to the early and mid-Victorian economy. **388** does not try to present any startling new conclusions—rather to interpret for the general reader the findings of the more specialised monographs. Although **389** examines the political reforms and social structure that were a concomitant of industrialisation, it is particularly strong in its economic history and contains an excellent chapter on the classical political economists. It admirably complements the analysis of **481**.

390. R. S. Sayers, *A history of economic change in England, 1880–1939* (1967)

391. W. Ashworth, *An economic history of England, 1870–1939* (1960)

392. D. H. Aldcroft and H. W. Richardson, *The British economy, 1870–1939* (1969)

It may well be symptomatic of our own age that depression rather than prosperity has fascinated recent historians. **390** is a short introduction which can be read before the fuller and more authoritative **391**. **392** has a useful first section which summarises developments in the period for the non-specialist, and includes a survey of statistical sources and a critical bibliography.

393. R. A. Church, *The great Victorian boom 1850–73* (1975)

394. S. B. Saul, *The myth of the great depression 1873–96* (1969)

Two volumes in the series 'Studies in economic and social history' [see **82**] which bear the general hallmarks of that series but are also atypical in that they are less concerned with summarising a historical debate than with questioning orthodox interpretations—the first that the mid-Victorian years were essentially a period of boom, the second that the later years were generally a period of depression.

395. E. M. Carus-Wilson (ed.), *Essays in economic history, vol. iii* (1962)

396. R. M. Hartwell, *The industrial revolution and economic growth* (1971)

397. D. H. Aldcroft and P. Fearon (eds.), *British economic fluctuations 1790–1939* (1972)

Collections of important articles, the majority of which have appeared in journals. Of Hartwell's essays, those which present his 'optimistic' interpretation of the standard-of-living in the early nineteenth century should be contrasted with the views of the 'pessimists' [see **655–56**].

398. P. Deane and W. A. Cole, *British economic growth 1688–1959: trends and structure* (1962; 2nd ed., 1967)

399. B. R. Mitchell, with P. Deane, *Abstract of British historical statistics* (1962)

398 attempts to tell the story of British economic development in quantitative terms and is a companion-volume to the statistical tables assembled in **399**. Some of the extrapolations from scanty evidence made in **398** for the period before reliable statistical information was collated have been questioned by other economic historians, but it is nonetheless a key book containing important information on the staple industries, population increase and changing labour patterns, and economic growth. **399** is the economic historian's bible of statistics—and their value and limitations are admirably described in the short introductions to each section.

Agriculture

400. R. E. Prothero (Lord Ernle), *English farming, past and present* (1912; 6th ed., with introductions by G. E. Fussell and O. R. McGregor, 1961)

401. J. D. Chambers and G. E. Mingay, *The agricultural revolution, 1750–1880* (1966)

402. C. S. Orwin and E. H. Whetham, *A history of British agriculture, 1846–1914* (1964)

Lord Ernle's pioneering study has deservedly been reprinted numerous times since it was first published over sixty years ago, and the 1961 edition, with the excellent introductions by Fussell and McGregor which draw attention to its deficiences as well as its strengths, is still one of the best agrarian histories. It must, of course, be supplemented with the fruits of more recent research, and **401** is now the standard work, though for the last quarter of the century one must either turn to the pedestrian account in **402** or the more stimulating thesis of **405**.

403. E. L. Jones, *The development of English agriculture, 1815–73* (1968)

404. E. L. Jones, *Agriculture and the industrial revolution* (1974)

403, in the 'Studies in economic and social history' series [see **82**], is a very good introduction to the literature on the subject, and **404**, a collection of journal-articles by Jones, a further source for his major essay 'The changing basis of English agricultural prosperity, 1853–73'.

405. P. J. Perry, *British farming in the great depression, 1870–1914* (1974)

406. P. J. Perry (ed.), *British agriculture 1875–1914* (1973)

Agrarian history, like most other branches of history, is benefiting from local studies which will ultimately change the overall general picture. Books such as **405**, which emphasises regional variations in the impact of the great depression, demonstrate the extent to which the standard theories need to be revised. **406** is a collection of articles with an introduction which summarises the arguments of **405**.

407. E. L. Jones, *Seasons and prices. The role of the weather in English agricultural history* (1964)

Deals with what is, at first glance, an apparently abstruse and minor topic—in fact quite the contrary. Agrarian historians in discussing improvements in machinery, or technique, or trends have tended to ignore the very important and ultimate dependence of agricultural production on the weather. A bad harvest due to inclement weather was, after all, a contributory cause of many riots in the nineteenth century (and, of course, earlier). Jones has rightly devoted a monograph to this significant aspect of agricultural history—significant for both the economic and the social historian.

408. W. E. Minchinton (ed.), *Essays in agrarian history, vol. ii* (1968)

A reprint of articles including an important one by T. W.

Fletcher on 'The great depression of English agriculture, 1873–96', and by Jones on agricultural prosperity [see **404**].

409. E. J. Evans, *The contentious tithe. The tithe problem and English agriculture, 1750–1850* (1976)
A short introduction to a neglected topic.

410. R. Douglas, *Land, people and politics. A history of the land question in the United Kingdom, 1878–1952* (1976)
A disappointing study of a subject which deserves a modern monograph. But Douglas retells the fairly familiar story of land legislation and the aspirations of radical reformers—the proponents of land taxation and nationalisation.

Industry

(a) GENERAL

411. S. Pollard, *The genesis of modern management: a study of the industrial revolution in Great Britain* (1965)

412. P. L. Payne, *British entrepreneurship in the nineteenth century* (1974)

413. R. H. Campbell and R. G. Wilson (eds.), *Entrepreneurship in Britain 1750–1939* (1975)
Generalisations about entrepreneurial activity have been based, as Payne argues in his excellent introduction to this subject in his contribution to the 'Studies in economic and social history' series [see **82**], on a paucity of monographs mainly of successful businesses. Pollard however, is able to make many valuable observations concerning the evolution of a managerial class in his comprehensive survey of the impact of industrialisation on organisational techniques. **413** is a short collection of extracts from the writings of entrepreneurs, economists, and government inspectors, prefaced by an extremely useful bibliographical essay.

414. A. L. Levine, *Industrial retardation in Britain 1880–1914* (1967)

415. D. H. Aldcroft (ed.), *The development of British industry and foreign competition, 1875–1914. Studies in industrial enterprise* (1968)
414 examines the role of management and of labour in, as well as some of the conventional explanations of, the phenomenon described in the title, and concludes that the response of British

entrepreneurship to innovations in industry was largely to blame for the retardation. But Aldcroft, in attempting to summarise the findings of the ten contributors to **415** who examined developments and the role of foreign competition in a number of major industries, was unable to draw any such firm conclusions as to the relative decline of the British economy.

(b) COAL MINING

416. B. Lewis, *Coal mining in the eighteenth and nineteenth centuries* (1971)

A brief guide to the subject—one of the 'Seminar studies' series [see **70**].

(c) COTTON DURING THE FAMINE

417. W. O. Henderson, *The Lancashire cotton famine 1861–65* (1934; 2nd ed., 1969)

418. M. Ellison, *Support for secession: Lancashire and the American civil war* (1973)

417, which includes an analysis of the state of the Lancashire cotton industry in 1860, has been the standard account of the economic and social aspects of the famine for over forty years. The picture of a Lancashire workforce bearing the hardships of the famine because of their sympathy and commitment to the antislavery cause is shown by **418** to be a caricature.

(d) NEWSPAPERS

419. H. Herd, *The march of journalism. The story of the British press from 1622 to the present day* (1952)

420. F. Williams, *Dangerous estate. The anatomy of newspapers* (1957)

Despite the large number of studies of the press and the histories of individual newspapers there is still no satisfactory general survey to replace H. Fox Bourne's two-volume history published in 1887. **419** is a very broad outline of the main developments, and **420** is itself a journalistic though highly readable account of the fourth estate.

421. D. Read, *Press and people 1790–1850: opinion in three English cities* (1961)

A suggestive sortie into provincial journalism (which deserves a fuller study). The three cities are Leeds, Sheffield and Manchester.

422. S. Harrison, *Poor men's guardians. A survey of the struggles for a democratic newspaper press 1763–1973* (1974)

423. A. Aspinall, *Politics and the press, c. 1780–1850* (1949)

424. W. H. Wickwar, *The struggle for the freedom of the press, 1819–32* (1928)

425. J. H. Wiener, *The war of the unstamped: a history of the movement to repeal the British newspaper tax, 1830–36* (1969)

426. P. Hollis, *The pauper press. A study of working-class radicalism of the 1830s* (1970)

427. A. J. Lee, *The origins of the popular press 1855–1914* (1976)

Six books which taken together provide a comprehensive account of the progress towards a free and popular press. **422** is the only overall survey written for the general reader. **423** is particularly good on the gradual dismantling of a pervasive political control. **424** is an old but still valuable account of the prosecution of the press in a period of intense radical activity. **426** continues this theme into the 1830s and the mushrooming of the unstamped press. It covers similar ground to **425** but the latter is more concerned with the campaign to repeal the so-called 'taxes on knowledge'. Lastly, **427** takes the story into the late nineteenth century by examining not only the struggles for a cheap press and the technological developments which made the exploitation of a large market possible, but also by assessing the impact of these and other changes on the earlier ideals and expectations of the campaigning Liberal reformers. [Cf. **168**].

(e) INDUSTRIAL ARCHAEOLOGY

428. M. Rix, *Industrial archaeology* (1967)

429. K. Hudson, *Industrial archaeology* (1963; 3rd ed., 1976)

430. R. A. Buchanan, *Industrial archaeology in Britain* (1972)

Industrial archaeology, the attempt to record, preserve and interpret the sites and structures of industrial activity, is a burgeoning subject, and David & Charles, for example, are engaged in publishing a large number of regional studies of the British Isles. But the three books mentioned here are good, short introductions for the general reader—the first an Historical Association pamphlet and the last a moderately priced paperback. Those who wish to place the subject in its wider historical context should turn to a general survey by A. Raistrick.

Overseas Trade and Investment
[see also, **56, 148,** and **328–30**]

431. W. Schlote, *British overseas trade. From 1700 to the 1930s* (1938; trans., 1952)

432. A. H. Imlah, *Economic elements in the Pax Britannica. Studies in British foreign trade in the nineteenth century* (1958)

433. S. B. Saul, *Studies in British overseas trade 1870–1914* (1960)

434. A. R. Hall (ed.), *The export of capital from Britain, 1870–1914* (1968)

431, which originally appeared in Germany in 1938 and was translated into English by W. O. Henderson and W. H. Chaloner in 1952, has now been largely superseded by the more reliable statistical analysis of **432,** though its account of the fluctuations and geographical distribution of trade is short enough to prolong its usefulness as an introduction. **432** is, indeed, the best general history of overseas trade and investment, and the transition from protection to free trade, but it needs to be supplemented with the excellent but more specialised studies contained in **433**. The articles reprinted in **434** contribute to the debate which links the export of capital through trade and investment to formal imperial domination [see **325–30**].

435. A. K. Cairncross, *Home and foreign investment, 1870–1913. Studies in capital accumulation* (1953)

436. P. L. Cottrell, *British overseas investment in the nineteenth century* (1975)

435 was among the first of a series of investigations, many of them like this one rather technical in approach, into the contribution of home and foreign investments to the strength of the British economy. Cottrell's volume in the 'Studies in economic and social history' series [see **82**] is a good summary of the conclusions of much of that research.

437. J. B. Williams, *British commercial policy and trade expansion, 1750–1850* (1972)

438. B. Turner, *Free trade and protection* (1971)

439. N. McCord (ed.), *Free trade: theory and practice from Adam Smith to Keynes* (1970)

The publication date of **437** disguises the fact that it was written in the 1950s—hence its apparent disregard for the conclusions of recent research into overseas trade. It does, however, contribute to our knowledge of government policy [and should be compared with **89**] and hence to our understanding of the early history of free trade. Turner's pamphlet in the 'Seminar' series [see **70**] summarises trade policy from corn law repeal to tariff reform, with a postscript on the postwar movement towards European economic unity. **433** is an anthology in the unsatisfactory 'Sources for social and economic history' series [see **738**].

Transport
[see also **299**]

(a) GENERAL

440. H. J. Dyos and D. H. Aldcroft, *British transport. An economic survey from the seventeenth century to the twentieth* (1969)

441. P. S. Bagwell, *The transport revolution from 1770* (1974)

442. T. C. Barker and C. I. Savage, *An economic history of transport in Britain* (1975)

440 and **441** are both excellent introductions to transport history bringing together the conclusions of recent research and presenting them in a manageable and highly readable form. As well as telling the familiar story of roads, railways, canals and ocean shipping, they include valuable sections on the occasionally neglected topic of coastal shipping. **440** also contains a very good bibliography. T. C. Barker has extended the short economic history of transport by the late C. I. Savage, published in 1959, and it is now a satisfactory alternative to **440** and **441**.

443. J. Simmons, *Transport* (1962)

Over two hundred illustrations and a relatively short text make this a popular introduction to transport history.

444. D. H. Aldcroft, *Studies in British transport history 1870–1970* (1974)

These essays are on the whole too specialised for the average undergraduate, but Aldcroft's introduction is an illuminating review of the current state of transport studies.

445. T. C. Barker and M. Robbins, *A history of London transport. Vol. i: the nineteenth century* (1963)

This first volume, written by Theo Barker, provides a sound

survey of the evolution of London transport from the horse bus to the underground. Its account of railway developments in the metropolis should be compared with the conclusions of **708**.

(b) RAILWAYS [see also, **88, 495, 567** and **708**]

446. C. H. Ellis, *British railway history: an outline from the accession of William IV to the nationalisation of railways* (2 vols., 1954–59)

447. J. Simmons, *The railways of Britain: an historical introduction* (1961)

448. M. Robbins, *The railway age* (1962)

Judging by the large number of histories of railways written from both a national and a local perspective, and the biographies of pioneers such as the Stephensons or Brunel, many men have not lost their childhood passion for steam traction. It is surprising, therefore, that we have had to wait until the 1950s for the first serious attempt at a comprehensive historical survey (**446**) but even this ignored the crucial interrelationship of railway expansion with economic growth. Since then we have had the short but scholarly introduction by Simmons, and the extended essay on railways in their social dimension by Robbins, as well as the much-needed economic histories considered immediately below.

449. M. C. Reed (ed.), *Railways in the Victorian economy. Studies in finance and economic growth* (1969)

450. G. R. Hawke, *Railways and economic growth in England and Wales, 1840–70* (1970)

451. S. Broadbridge, *Studies in railway expansion and the capital market in England, 1825–73* (1970)

452. H. Pollins, *Britain's railways: an industrial history* (1971)

The statistical tables in these specialised monographs on railways and the economy make for heavy reading. Some students will find the use of economic concepts and mathematical analysis in **450** especially hard to digest, but should look at this book as an example of the application of econometrics to British railway history. The rest are more orthodox in approach. The collection of essays in **449** includes a crucial one by B. R. Mitchell on the contribution of railways to the growth of the Victorian economy; **451** uses the records of the Lancashire and Yorkshire Railway Company to examine the role of the individual companies; and **452** draws together the conclusions of much of the recent research.

453. G. Alderman, *The railway interest* (1973)

A perceptive study of the growth of pressure-group activities by the railway companies following government intervention in terms of passenger rates and safety regulations. Of value to the political as well as the economic historian.

Trade Unions and Labour Relations

454. S. J. & B. Webb, *The history of trade unionism* (1894; 2nd ed., 1920)

455. H. Pelling, *A history of British trade unionism* (1963)

456. A. Hutt, *British trade unionism. A short history* (1941; 6th ed., 1975)

Sidney and Beatrice Webb's pioneering history is still standard reading despite its age and the fact that some of its conclusions have been overturned by later research. It should be used in close conjunction with Pelling's concise and competent but rather flat survey. Hutt's Marxist outline history is more zestful but oversimplified.

457. A. E. Musson, *British trade unions 1800–75* (1972)

458. W. H. Fraser, *Trade unions and society: the struggle for acceptance, 1850–80* (1974)

459. H. A. Clegg, A. Fox, and A. F. Thompson, *A history of British trade unions since 1889. Vol. i: 1889–1910* (1964)

Trade-union growth in the latter half of the nineteenth century can be comprehensively studied by using **458** and **459**, albeit the detail of the latter tends to obscure trends in development. There is still scope, however, for an up-to-date monograph on unionism in the early Victorian period, although **457** in the series 'Studies in economic and social history' [see **82**] reviews the literature that is available and itself provides a temporary stop-gap. [As does W. H. Fraser's essay in **587**.]

460. A. E. Musson, *The congress of 1868: the origins and establishment of the trades union congress* (1955)

461. J. C. Lovell and B. C. Roberts, *A short history of the T.U.C.* (1968)

462. B. C. Roberts, *The trades union congress, 1868–1921* (1958)

460 and **461** are little more than bare outlines but **462** is a full history of the congress from its origins to the establishment of the general council.

463. H. A. Turner, *Trade union growth, structure, and policy: a comparative study of the cotton unions* (1962)
His analysis of the origins and workings of the cotton unions forms the basis for a general set of theoretical speculations on the growth of trade unions. Some basic knowledge is required before approaching this book, and it is no substitute for the much-needed study of trade unionism in the cotton industry. [But see **477**.]

464. G. E. Fussell, *From Tolpuddle to T.U.C. A century of farm labourers' politics* (1948)

465. R. Groves, *Sharpen the sickle! The history of the Farm Workers' Union* (1949)

466. P. Horn, *Joseph Arch, 1826–1919: the farmworkers' leader* (1971)
464 and 465 were written at about the same time and tread much the same ground. 466 is interesting as much for its account of Arch's leadership of the farm labourers' agitation and its economic background as it is for his subsequent decline into the curious status of a respectable alcoholic. [See also, **546–54**.]

467. R. Challinor and B. Ripley, *The Miners' Association: a trade union in the age of the Chartists* (1968)

468. R. Page Arnot, *The miners. A history of the Miners' Federation of Great Britain, 1889–1910* (1949)
The story of mining unionism has been quite extensively narrated and, apart from these two general studies, there are regional histories for example of the miners of Derbyshire, Nottinghamshire, Yorkshire, Northumberland and Durham, South Wales, the Forest of Dean, and Lancashire and Cheshire. [See also, **198** and **568**.]

469. J. B. Jefferys, *The story of the engineers, 1800–1945* (1946)
Although written a generation ago this account has not been superseded.

470. P. S. Bagwell, *The railwaymen. The history of the National Union of Railwaymen* (1963)

471. P. W. Kingsford, *Victorian railwaymen: the emergence and growth of a railway labour 1830–70* (1970)
The first section of **470** is a painstaking narrative of the Amalgamated Society of Railway Servants, a forerunner of the N.U.R. By

contrast **471** is as much a piece of social as of economic history, concerned with the background from which the railways drew their recruits, but it would have benefited greatly from some analysis of the information so carefully gathered together.

472. J. C. Lovell, *Stevedores and dockers: a study of trade unionism in the Port of London, 1870–1914* (1971)

Brings out clearly the difficulties involved in organising a hybrid workforce of skilled stevedores and casual dock labourers.

473. R. Hyman, *The Workers' Union* (1971)

The history of the Workers' Union, founded in 1898 in an attempt to recruit hitherto non-unionised groups, had not, until the publication of this book, received the attention from historians which it deserved. It was, after all, the second largest union by 1919, though its membership thereafter declined quite rapidly.

474. R. and E. Frow and M. Katanka (eds.), *Strikes. A documentary history* (1971)

A collection of documents covering the years 1756 to 1926. Its brief introduction is primarily a potted history of strike-action rather than an informative guide to the extracts it contains.

475. A. Stafford, *A match to fire the Thames* (1961)

An uncritical narrative of the new unionism of 1888–89. The two essays on the subject in **181** are far better.

476. P. S. Bagwell, *Industrial relations: government and society in nineteenth-century Britain* (1974)

477. K. Burgess, *The origins of British industrial relations: the nineteenth-century experience* (1975)

478. E. H. Phelps Brown, *The growth of British industrial relations. A study from the standpoint of 1906–14* (1959)

476 is ostensibly a guide to the Irish University Press's publication of British parliamentary papers, but it is more than that. The bulk of the book is a 'commentary' synopsis of trade-union history incorporating the conclusions of recent research, followed by an excellent selection from the parliamentary papers, and a full bibliography. Basing his thinking on a study of the engineering, building, coal mining and cotton industries, Burgess finds the origins of modern industrial relations in the last quarter of the nineteenth century. By contrast, **478** is an important study of the background to, and the disappearance of, the strife in industrial relations which characterised the immediate pre-war period.

479. G. W. Hilton, *The truck system, including a history of the British Truck Acts, 1465–1960* (1960)

480. E. H. Hunt, *Regional wage variations in Britain 1850–1914* (1973)

There have been very few general studies of the wages aspect of labour relations. The questions raised in Hunt's tentative examination of regional differences need to be further explored by historians. **479** is, however, a comprehensive account of the nefarious practice of payment by 'truck' instead of money wages and the ineffectiveness of nineteenth-century legislation in stamping it out.

5
SOCIAL

The content of history syllabuses has changed quite considerably over the last ten or twenty years. The most substantial development has been the trend away from political and constitutional, and towards more social, history. The latter is no longer defined as the study of customs, fashions, or manners (though there is still much trivial writing on these subjects), nor is it simply, in G. M. Trevelyan's oft-quoted remark, history with the politics left out. Rather, it is an attempt to progress towards that presentation of a composite view of society I described earlier—progress made possible by the exertions since the war of an energetic band of labour historians, and, latterly, by a heartening growth in awareness among British historians of the utility to their discipline of social theory and concepts drawn from sociology. Quaint accounts of village and working lives are being replaced by the quintessential social history of the History Workshop [see **549** and **568**, and Appendix B]; the middle classes are enjoying a revival; and antiquarian and parish-pump local histories are being superseded by the products of scholars busily beavering away at the new urban history.

Publishers have responded by making inaccessible texts more readily available. The Leicester University Press through its 'Victorian Library' series has reprinted an interesting range of titles, edited by distinguished historians, and offered at a price which is not prohibitive. Among these are such classics as W. Lovett and J. Collins's *Chartism: a new organization of the people*; G. A. Sala's *Twice round the clock*; and A. Mearns's *The bitter cry of outcast London*. The Harvester Press have reproduced some important material in microform—for example, the full seventeen volumes of Charles Booth's *Life and labour of the people in London*—as well as reprinting a number of important contemporary texts in their series 'Society and the Victorians'. Frank Cass & Co. and the Woburn Press have for some years now been prominent in the reprinting of a great deal of Victorian material at a low price. The 'Cass library of Victorian times' and the Woburn series 'The social history of education' and 'Studies in urban history' are particularly relevant. Lastly, the now-discontinued Gregg International's 'Victorian conscience' series has made available several volumes of facsimile reprints of articles on social problems from prominent nineteenth-century journals, again introduced by a specialist historian. Much of the material issued by these publishers is too voluminous and also a little too specialised for inclusion here; those interested should consult their catalogues.

General
[see also, **375–78** and **389**]

481. H. Perkin, *The origins of modern English society 1780–1880* (1969)

482. J. Ryder and H. Silver, *Modern English society: history and structure 1850–1970* (1970; 2nd ed., 1977)

483. J. Roebuck, *The making of modern English society from 1850* (1973)

The similarity between these books ends with the titles. **481** is a sophisticated analysis of the emergence of industrial society, probably intended as a non-Marxist response to **559**, alongside which it should most certainly be read. It is well-written, lively, stimulating and, above all, controversial though at times over-generalised. Its substitution of 'ideals' (such as the 'entrepreneurial ideal') for basic clashes of class interest in its promulgation of the *embourgeoisement* thesis [cf. **586**] tends in some respects to obscure rather than to clarify the issues, but even in this it is thought-provoking. The same cannot be said for the elementary level of **483** which is unlikely to satisfy the developed intellect. **482** is a novel attempt to look at the growth of modern society first through the eyes of the historian and then through the eyes of the sociologist, rather than an integration of the two disciplines in the manner of **481**.

484. G. M. Trevelyan, *Illustrated English social history. Vol. iv: the nineteenth century* (1952)

485. D. C. Somervell, *The Victorian age* (1937)

486. C. A. Petrie, *The Victorians* (1960)

487. H. and M. Evans, *The Victorians at home and at work as illustrated by themselves* (1973)

488. N. Bentley, *The Victorian scene, a picture book of the period 1837–1901* (1968)

The social life of the Victorians has exercised the curiosity of historians ever since the reaction set in against Lytton Strachey's acid criticisms. This antiquarian fascination has produced a large body of ephemeral literature best forgotten. **487**, for example, is one of the most recent, and one of the worst, of this type of history; and **486**, though agreeably written and spiced with wit, ignores the progress in historical scholarship since the second world war. But the better side of this tradition has produced such beautifully illustrated and entertaining history as **484** and **488**, or the early and succinct contribution to the now hoary old debate as to whether one can talk of a 'Victorian' age—the Historical Association pamphlet, **485**.

489. R. J. White, *Life in Regency England* (1963)

490. W. J. Reader, *Life in Victorian England* (1964)

491. R. Cecil, *Life in Edwardian England* (1969)

Three popular, light, and well-illustrated introductions to the social history of the nineteenth century in the 'English life series' edited by P. Quennell, but no substitute for the three books which follow.

492. J. F. C. Harrison, *The early Victorians, 1832–51* (1971)

493. G. F. A. Best, *Mid-Victorian Britain, 1851–75* (1971)

494. P. Thompson, *The Edwardians. The remaking of British society* (1975)

Three superlative pieces of historical writing. Although they all belong to the same series—'The making of modern British society' edited by E. J. Hobsbawm—they are different in both style and content, yet each is excellent in its own way. Harrison's is more obviously a work of summary and synthesis, the logical outcome of the sixties' trend in the writing of social history, concerned with the structure and interplay of a class society. Best, too, has been influenced by this trend, but at the same time is linked to an earlier tradition—a G. M. Young suddenly thrust bodily into the 1970s. The statistics are there; the analysis of social structure is there; the provincial cities get their due place. But above all and through all shines Best's thorough mastery, and, most important, love of his subject—the ability to convey to the reader what it must have been like to live in mid-Victorian Britain (and not, incidentally, just England). Thompson's book reflects an even more recent trend—the attempt largely pioneered by the History Workshop to recreate the lives of ordinary working-class men and women. The accumulation of oral evidence has been its most significant methodological departure, and by using such evidence to throw Edwardian society into relief Thompson has largely avoided oral history's most dangerous pitfall—ultra-empiricism. If the forthcoming volume on the late nineteenth century matches these three in quality, then the series must surely become the standard introduction to the period.

495. H. Perkin, *The age of the railway* (1971)

Based on a television series and aimed at the popular market, this is nevertheless solid social history centring on, but by no means confined to, the impact of the railways particularly in respect of changes in leisure, and summarising some of the conclusions of his more serious analysis [**481**].

496. R. Pearsall, *Edwardian life and leisure* (1973)

A popular, predominantly social, history of the years 1901–14, out of touch with serious historical research and misleading in its bald statements and over-generalisations. It does, however, contain some good illustrations.

497. W. E. Houghton, *The Victorian frame of mind, 1830–70* (1957)

498. G. B. Kauvar and G. C. Sorensen (eds.), *The Victorian mind* (1969)

499. S. L. Hynes, *The Edwardian turn of mind* (1968)

Three books which attempt the impossible—an analysis of the mind of an age—but **497** and **499** are to be congratulated for making the attempt, for if they have not succeeded they have certainly produced much food for thought. **498** is an anthology which brings out the controversy among Victorians on such subjects as education, social welfare, religion, science, and art.

500. R. D. Altick, *Victorian people and ideas* (1973)

501. *Ideas and beliefs of the Victorians* (1949)

500 is intended as a literature student's guide to the social and intellectual history of the Victorian age and it draws heavily on literary sources. But as a piece of historical portraiture it is stereotyped and unoriginal, and the student would be well-advised to seek his 'background' elsewhere. **501** is a collection of B.B.C. broadcasts on such themes as the family, sex, wealth, women, social conscience and Liberalism, subjects of much subsequent research. The book was reissued in America in 1966 and might also profitably be brought back into print in Britain.

502. A. Briggs, *1851* (1951)

503. W. N. Medlicott (ed.), *From Metternich to Hitler. Aspects of British and foreign history 1814-1939* (1963)

504. G. M. Young, *Victorian essays* (1962)

Briggs's centenary portrait of life in 1851 and Somervell's Victorian age [**485**] are included in the collection of Historical Association essays reprinted in **503**. Young's essays are, arguably, history at its most empirical and trivial, but certainly liberal history at its most colourful, witty and best. See, for example, his essays entitled 'Victorian centenary' and 'The greatest Victorian'. Those who wish to know his candidate for the latter title will have to read the essays for themselves!

505. M. W. Flinn and T. C. Smout (eds.), *Essays in social history* (1974)

506. J. Butt and I. F. Clarke (eds.), *The Victorians and social protest: a symposium* (1973)

505 is a reprint of twelve excellent articles—it would be invidious to single out any one for particular attention, the whole volume is a model of its type. This is not true of **506**, the six essays of which are uneven in quality and of uncertain relevance to the title of the symposium. The most important is undoubtedly Perkin's on land reform.

507. C. Bolt, *Victorian attitudes to race* (1971)

Standing virtually alone in attempting a comparative survey of Victorian attitudes to coloured peoples, she raises questions which deserve further exploration.

508. R. Pearsall, *Night's black angels: the forms and faces of Victorian cruelty* (1975)

Draws together from diverse secondary sources facts about cruelty familiar to most students of the period. He describes, for example, flogging in the public schools, conditions in mines and factories, and in the armed services and the prisons, cruelty to animals, sexual deviancy, prostitution and white slavery. Unfortunately, the book never moves from the particular to the general. It wallows in the sensational detail without asking questions concerning the prevalence of certain types of cruelty. And where it does make general statements they are not to be trusted—he concludes, for example, that flagellation was 'the English vice'!

509. E. R. Pike (ed.), *Human documents of the industrial revolution in Britain* (1966)

Social

510. E. R. Pike (ed.), *Human documents of the Victorian golden age (1850–70)* (1967)

511. E. R. Pike (ed.), *Human documents of the age of the Forsytes* (1969)

512. E. R. Pike (ed.), *Human documents of the Lloyd George era* (1972)

513. E. C. Black (ed.), *Victorian culture and society* (1973)

514. J. H. Wiener (ed.), *Great Britain: the lion at home. A documentary history of domestic policy 1689–1973* (4 vols., 1974)

515. J. F. C. Harrison (ed.), *Society and politics in England, 1780–1960: a selection of readings and comments* (1965)

516. J. T. Ward (ed.), *The age of change, 1770–1870. Documents in social history* (1975)

There is certainly no shortage of readily available documentary material for classroom use. The value of short extracts is debatable, and the extent to which they are used is a matter of personal taste. Certainly Pike's four volumes are more useful for the documents than for the comments. **513** is a companion to **47**, and **514**, the first three volumes of which contain material on the nineteenth century, to **310**. Approximately half of **515** appertains to the nineteenth century. Its documents are drawn from reasonably accessible printed sources—such as Bagehot [**40**] or Chadwick [referred to at **676**]—with the aim of introducing the student to these key works. And **516** is yet one more selection of short extracts and even shorter comments.

517. C. F. G. Masterman, *The condition of England* (1909; new ed., 1960)

A perceptive contemporary analysis of Edwardian society.

Population

518. N. Tranter, *Population since the industrial revolution: the case of England and Wales* (1973)

519. M. W. Flinn, *British population growth, 1700–1850* (1970)

520. H. J. Habakkuk, *Population growth and economic development since 1750* (1971)

518 is a most important textbook on English demography in the industrial age though it must be supplemented with studies of internal migration [for example, **531** and **532**] and urban growth [for example, chapter one of **706**]. However, a short and excellent introduction to population increase in the early part of our period is **519** in the 'Studies in economic and social history' series [see **82**]. Some of the points raised in both these books—particularly concerning the chicken-and-egg conundrum of the relationship between population and economic growth—are developed in the lectures printed in **520**. [See also, the essay on mortality-rates by McKeown and Record in **505**, and McKeown's more general treatise on *The modern rise of population*.]

521. D. C. Marsh, *The changing social structure of England and Wales, 1871–1961* (1958; new ed., 1965)

522. N. J. Smelser, *Social change in the industrial revolution. An application of theory to the Lancashire cotton industry 1770–1840* (1959)

523. M. Anderson, *Family structure in nineteenth-century Lancashire* (1971)

Three sociological surveys of population growth and structure. Indeed, there has been much recent work on family structure, for example by P. Laslett, E. Shorter and others. **521**'s analysis of changing family size, regional variations, occupations, classes, educational opportunities and social problems is at times over-simplified, but it is nevertheless an excellent introduction to the subject. Although **522** is not confined solely to the changes in family structure wrought by the industrial revolution, the sections of the book which deal with this important subject are certainly the best. They must, however, be compared with the minute analysis, based largely on a study of Preston, in **523**. The sociological jargon employed in the latter will tax those history undergraduates with a traditional 'arts' training, and, indeed, Anderson advises non-sociologists to skim through his theoretical chapters. But the book is indicative of the trend in historical studies towards the fuller employment of analytical concepts, and future students will have to master these tools of the sociologist's trade in the same way as economics forced past students to master precise quantification.

524. E. A. Wrigley (ed.), *Nineteenth-century society: essays in the use of quantitative methods for the study of social data* (1972)

The title of this collection of essays is misleading in that they are primarily concerned with demonstrating how one source for the demographer, the census returns, can be put to good use. Anderson discusses the methodology employed in writing **523**, and V. A. C.

Gattrell and T. B. Hadden examine criminal statistics. Other demographers, such as D. V. Glass, have also provided guides to the use and development of population-statistics.

525. J. A. Banks, *Prosperity and parenthood. A study of family planning among the Victorian middle classes* (1954)

526. J. A. and O. Banks, *Feminism and family planning in Victorian England* (1964)

527. P. Fryer, *The birth-controllers* (1965)

The Banks's pioneering studies examine the extent to which the decline in the rate of population increase in late Victorian England was related to the rise in living standards and the growth of feminism. Many of the questions they raise require further exploration. Fryer's book is primarily valuable for its biographical details on the early advocates of birth-control.

528. O. R. McGregor, *Divorce in England: a centenary study* (1947)

A well-balanced account of just one aspect of changing family structure in an industrial society. His chapter on the Victorian family sweeps away many hitherto ill-founded assumptions. While his work on divorce has been followed up, his account of legal separation has not.

529. J. Morley, *Death, heaven and the Victorians* (1971)

530. J. S. Curl, *The Victorian celebration of death* (1972)

It is often remarked that while the Victorians talked of death but not of sex the conversational preoccupations of recent generations have been exactly the reverse. The activities of historians certainly bears out this general observation for while the sexual proclivities of the Victorians attracted their eager attention, until quite recently there were no serious studies of the Victorian 'celebration' of death. Even now these two books mark only a tentative beginning. **529**, for example, is a serious and well-illustrated study of four aspects of the question: a debate on funerals in the 1840s; the Duke of Wellington's funeral in 1852; the cremation movement which began in the 1870s; and the spiritualist movement. Curl's is a popular illustrated volume largely concerned with funerals, cemeteries and cremation in the London metropolitan area. Unfortunately, neither say very much about the 'economics' of death—after all, the funeral industry must have been a sizeable slice of the Victorian economy.

531. A. Redford, *Labour migration in England 1800–50* (1926; 3rd ed., 1976)

532. J. Saville, *Rural depopulation in England and Wales 1851–1951* (1957)

Two studies which together survey internal migration during the whole of the nineteenth century. The excellent older study by Redford justly deserves its recent new edition and the first two chapters of **532** are a sound introduction to the factors underlying rural depopulation.

533. H. J. M. Johnston, *British emigration policy, 1815–30. 'Shovelling out the paupers'* (1972)

There are several studies of emigration, some related to the movement to specific areas of the world. This is the most recent and is particularly valuable because it concentrates on government policy, albeit within a very limited period. It therefore contributes to the MacDonagh–Parris debate [see **85**].

534. L. P. Gartner, *The Jewish immigrant in England, 1870–1914* (1960)

535. J. A. Garrard, *The English and immigration: a comparative study of the Jewish influx, 1880–1910* (1971)

536. B. Gainer, *The alien invasion: the origins of the Aliens Act of 1905* (1972)

534 is an impressive chronicle of Jewish immigration and life within the newly-formed Jewish communities, whereas **535** concentrates in a somewhat spotty study on the political and social reaction to the influx in the wake of the depression. Gainer's conclusions do not differ in any marked way from those advanced by Garrard, but he writes in a far more authoritative way and his sources are more fully documented.

537. J. A. Jackson, *The Irish in Britain* (1963)

538. L. P. Curtis Jr., *Anglo-Saxon and Celts: a study of Anglo-Irish prejudice in Victorian England* (1968)

539. L. P. Curtis Jr., *Apes and angels: the Irishman in Victorian caricature* (1971)

537 is a meticulous study of the most substantial minority group in nineteenth-century Britain, especially important for its analysis of the influence of post-famine immigrants on the labour movement and on the position of the Roman Catholic church. [Cf. **794**.] Curtis's discussion of the 'Paddy factor' (**538**) in Anglo-Irish relations is less useful than the book's title suggests, but a little better than his more recent study (**539**) of cartoon caricatures of the Irish.

Rural Society

[for the economic background, see under 'Agriculture' in Section 4]

(a) GENERAL

540. G. E. Mingay, *Rural life in Victorian England* (1976)
Largely a work of synthesis drawing heavily on secondary sources to present a general account of all levels of Victorian rural society.

541. W. Cobbett, *Rural rides* . . . (2 vols., 1830; 1 vol. ed., with intro. by G. Woodcock, 1967)
Classic description of rural southern England in the 1820s as well as a prime source for the idiosyncratic views of this ebullient radical—not least his unswervingly stubborn refusal to believe that the English population was increasing as a result of the industrial revolution. It is interesting to compare Cobbett's account with Rider Haggard's description of rural England at the start of the twentieth century, though the latter's book is not readily available.

(b) THE LANDED CLASSES

542. F. M. L. Thompson, *English landed society in the nineteenth century* (1963)

543. D. Spring, *The English landed estate in the nineteenth century: its administration* (1963)
These two books, published at almost the same time, throw interesting light upon the way of life of the landed elite. 543 is the narrower of the two, concerned as it is with the day-to-day management of an estate. On the other hand, Thompson charts the response of landed society to the seismic social and economic changes started by industrialisation, and is thus the more valuable as an undergraduate textbook. Work still remains to be done, however, on the subject of tenant farming.

544. J. T. Ward and R. G. Wilson (eds.), *Land and industry. The landed estate and the industrial revolution: a symposium* (1971)
The extent to which the class conflict diagnosed by Marx was obviated in Britain by the interfusion of the landed and industrial classes (socially and economically by, for example, marriage, the buying of land by industrialists and the exploitation of coal or railway contracts by landowners) is a theme which requires serious investigation by historians. [See, however, the excellent analysis by Barrington Moore in the chapters on England in his *Social origins of dictatorship*

and democracy]. The contributors to this symposium have begun to unravel the thread.

545. G. E. Mingay, *The gentry. The rise and fall of a ruling class* (1976)

A general survey of the gentry from the Norman Conquest to the present day, relying to some extent on secondary sources such as Thompson [542] for information on the nineteenth century.

(c) THE VILLAGE LABOURER

546. W. Hasbach, *A history of the English agricultural labourer* (1908; repr. 1966)

547. J. L. & B. Hammond, *The village labourer, 1760–1832* (1911; repr., 1966)

Hasbach's classic account of agricultural labour was first published in Germany in 1894 and has still not been superseded. The Hammonds' history is less reliable though it still provides useful background to the Swing riots. Their analysis of the latter has, however, been replaced by **554**.

548. F. Thompson, *Lark Rise to Candleford* (1945; repr., 1973)

Nostalgia for lost childhood and a lost way of life has been the frequent inspiration of autobiographical reminiscence. This recollection of Oxfordshire village life in the late nineteenth century is an excellent contribution to that *genre*.

549. R. Samuel (ed.), *Village life and labour* (1975)

550. P. Horn, *Labouring life in the Victorian countryside* (1976)

549 is a fine example of the new labour history, its commitment to resurrecting the lives of ordinary people through their own accounts (either oral or contemporary written) counterbalancing the empiricism which such a method invites. Hopefully, a new analysis will be possible at a future date. **550** is not it—though it does provide a fair synthesis of present knowledge of such themes as home life, school, crafts, wages, holidays, religion, sickness, poverty and crime in the Victorian countryside. Both books are beautifully illustrated with contemporary photographs.

551. J. P. D. Dunbabin, *Rural discontent in nineteenth-century Britain* (1975)

There is as yet no full survey of the changing forms of village protest in nineteenth-century Britain, but this is a promising beginning. The bulk of it is by Dunbabin (including chapters on Scottish crofting and Welsh anti-tithe movements) but there are also contributions by Pamela Horn on agricultural trade unionism in Oxfordshire and by A. J. Peacock on village radicalism in East Anglia in the first half of the century. Those who tread new ground often tread too much of it, and the contributors to this volume are no exception. But the detail of the middle chapters is mitigated by the early introductory ones and the last three on ideas, arguments and conclusions.

552. A. J. Peacock, *Bread or blood: a study of the agrarian riots in East Anglia in 1816* (1965)

553. R. C. Russell, *The 'revolt of the field' in Lincolnshire* (1956)

554. E. J. Hobsbawm and G. Rudé, *Captain Swing* (1969)

Three very good studies of rural disturbances, from the compelling narrative of the first to the succinct analysis of the causes and aftermath of the Swing riots in the last. The local study of the upsurge of agricultural trade unionism in Lincolnshire in the 1870s throws fresh light on that movement and is indicative of the gaps that still need to be plugged in the history of the rural proletariat, particularly between 1830 and 1870.

Urban Society

(a) THE MIDDLE CLASSES

555. A. M. Carr-Saunders and P. A. Wilson, *The professions* (1933; repr. 1964)

556. W. J. Reader, *Professional men: the rise of the professional classes in nineteenth-century England* (1966)

557. G. Crossick (ed.), *The lower-middle class in Britain 1870–1914* (1977)

558. G. Anderson, *Victorian clerks* (1976)

In terms of historical scholarship the middle classes have been neglected. For the past twenty-five years the field has been dominated by labour historians and, until recently, only the professional middle classes had received anything like the detailed treatment required. **555** is still the fullest study in this respect. It examines each major profession in turn, looks at the historical growth of professional groups, considers some of the criteria of 'professionalism', and, in a concluding section, speculates on the place of professionalism in a future society. Reader's later book on the same theme is shorter, derivative, but certainly more trenchant and readable. **557**, a collection of essays by a new group of historians (Geoffrey Crossick, Hugh McLeod, Richard Price, Greg Anderson, Robert Gray, Martin Gaskell, Thea Vigne and Alun Howkins), is indicative of a new direction in social history, and the subjects which they consider in relation to the lower-middle class, for example, religion, patriotism, culture, housing, shopkeeping, are likely to be developed at length in later studies—as, indeed, Anderson has already done for the Victorian clerks (**558**).

(b) THE WORKING CLASSES

559. E. P. Thompson, *The making of the English working class* (1963)

Thompson's controversial analysis of the emergence of working-class consciousness has already attained the status of a classic. He has opened up the whole of the period from 1780 to 1832 to new questions and new lines of approach, and his critics have been forced back to their desks to produce their own theories [see, for example, **481**]. The resultant lively and stimulating debate still shows few signs of flagging.

560. F. Engels, *The condition of the working class in England in 1844* (1845; trans., 1892)

561. S. Marcus, *Engels, Manchester, and the working class* (1974)

Whether Engels's celebrated description of the bleak industrial landscape of Manchester and its environs was exaggerated or not is contested in the two modern editions of his book—by W. H. Chaloner and W. O. Henderson (1958) and E. J. Hobsbawm (1969). **561** is essentially a literary critic's appraisal of Engels's book which also admonishes Chaloner and Henderson for their attacks on its usefulness. [See also, Hobsbawm's essay 'History and the "dark satanic mills"', in **181**; and Marcus's earlier and shorter piece in **706**].

562. J. L. and B. Hammond, *The town labourer, 1760–1832. The new civilisation* (1917; repr. 1966)

563. J. L. and B. Hammond, *The skilled labourer, 1760–1832* (1919; repr. 1965)

564. M. I. Thomis, *The town labourer and the industrial revolution* (1974)

The Hammonds' classic trilogy [for the third volume, see **547**] of labouring life presented a 'pessimistic' account of social conditions in the early industrial period. They wrote with a passionate sense of the wrongs which the working class endured in the formative period of industrial capitalism, and were not innocent of emotive bias. But Thomis's own assessment of their description of town labour is not so much a corrective as an ill-judged indictment evidenced in such naive statements as—'But the spies were really no-one's fault. They just happened at this time.'

565. P. Horn, *The rise and fall of the Victorian servant* (1975)

566. T. M. McBride, *The domestic revolution. The modernization of household service in England and France 1820–1920* (1976)

Domestic service, the largest employer of labour in the Victorian economy, has long required the serious consideration which it is only just beginning to receive partly as a spin-off from feminist studies and possibly from the popularity of television series such as *Upstairs downstairs*. Unfortunately, neither of these accounts goes much beyond a description of why women entered service, the duties they performed, and their expectations from the job, though **566** does contain illuminating comparisons of service in England and France, and comparative studies of this sort are indicative of a new trend in social history. But we still need to know more about servants as a class, including some analysis of their place in the social hierarchy particularly in relation to other working-class groups. [See also, **569**.]

567. T. Coleman, *The railway navvies* (1965)

Like the servants, the navvies were something of an exceptional group within the working class, and Coleman has written an entertaining account of a unique phase in social history. Those who enjoy reading Coleman may also delight in a socio-economic history of the canal boatmen by H. Hanson.

568. R. Samuel (ed.), *Miners, quarrymen and saltworkers* (1977)

The second in the History Workshop series, this account of coalminers, Welsh slate quarrymen and Cheshire saltworkers bears all the hallmarks of the first [see **549**].

569. J. Burnett (ed.), *Useful toil: autobiographies of working people from the 1820s to the 1920s* (1974)

Selections from the autobiographies of labourers, domestic servants and skilled workers. Most of the extracts are too short to do more than whet the appetite, but Burnett's introduction to each section places them soundly in context.

570. H. Mayhew, *London labour and the London poor* (4 vols., 1861–62; repr. 1968; 1 vol., ed. J. L. Bradley, 1965)

571. E. P. Thompson and E. Yeo (eds.), *The unknown Mayhew* (1971)

Mayhew's pungent descriptions of working-class life in Victorian London are the nineteenth-century equivalent of oral history—though one must confess his proneness to elaboration. But the view that his writings were impressionistic and his methods unscientific is effectively dismissed by Eileen Yeo in her introduction to the extracts from Mayhew's letters which appeared in the *Morning Chronicle*, 1849–50 (**571**), and his life and importance are finely assessed by both Bradley (**570**) and Thompson (**571**). No student can fail to savour Mayhew's fascinating account of by-gone street-life, especially his description of such ingenious occupations as the painting of drab birds to sell as tropical rarities, or the collection and purveyance to leather tanners of dog-droppings. The latter, incidentally, were used by bookbinders to cure their leather—a cautionary tale for all bibliophiles!

572. S. Pollard, *A history of labour in Sheffield* (1959)

This socio-economic history of the working class in a provincial city, primarily in the period after 1850, has surprisingly not been followed up by more local studies.

573. P. H. J. H. Gosden, *The friendly societies in England, 1815–75* (1961)

574. P. H. J. H. Gosden, *Self-help: voluntary associations in nineteenth-century Britain* (1974)

573 is the only major modern study of these important organisations of working-class thrift. Gosden's excursion into other aspects of self-help is rather less satisfactory, summarising his earlier writing on the friendly societies, describing burial societies, savings banks, cooperatives, building societies and so on, but failing to draw conclusions about their role in working-class culture.

(c) CLASS RELATIONSHIPS

575. R. S. Neale, *Class and ideology in the nineteenth century* (1972)

Contains excellent observations on nineteenth-century class-structure and posits a five-class model. [Cf. the essay by Briggs reprinted in both **179** and **505**.] G. D. H. Cole was a pioneer in this, as in so many other aspects of labour history, and some of the early chapters of his general studies in class structure, published in 1955, are still worth consulting.

576. P. Hollis (ed.), *Class and conflict in nineteenth-century England, 1815–50* (1973)

A collection of extracts from documents in Routledge's 'Birth of modern Britain' series (distributed in North America by the same publisher), the aim of which is 'to make the central issues and topics of the recent past "live", in both senses of that word'. In this case the main theme is the growth of working-class consciousness but Hollis's introduction and guide to further reading fall below the general standard of the series.

577. J. Foster, *Class struggle and the industrial revolution: early industrial capitalism in three English towns* (1974)

578. D. Fraser, *Urban politics in Victorian England* (1976)

Contrasting assessments of the level of class consciousness in a number of industrial towns. Foster applies E. P. Thompson's thesis concerning the formation of working-class consciousness [see **559**] to the test-case of Oldham and seeks to explain why the revolutionary promise of the 1830s and 1840s vanished with the 1850s. His book is particularly important for the new and rigorous methodology it employs. [See also, Foster's essay in **505** and compare his views with those of Tholfsen in **586**.] By contrast Fraser, basing his evidence primarily on developments in Manchester, Leeds, Liverpool and Birmingham, does not see class consciousness crystallising until the late nineteenth century when it manifested itself in the creation of a Labour party, but rather regards the urban scene in mid-century as a canvas for rivalry between middle-class elites. More than this though, his book demonstrates the great importance with which middle-class Victorians regarded parish-pump politics and is a significant contribution to the historiography of local government. [Cf. also, **123** and **303**.]

579. G. Stedman Jones, *Outcast London. A study in the relationship between classes in Victorian society* (1971)

A penetrating analysis of the casual labour problem in London's East End and middle-class attempts at amelioration.

580. D. Hudson, *Munby, man of two worlds: the life and diaries of Arthur J. Munby 1828–1910* (1972)

The two worlds between which Munby floated were those of his own middle-class circle and the working-class world of Hannah, the servant-girl whom he secretly married. His diaries, which make intriguing reading, relate his curious fascination with brawny, working women, and the story of his clandestine relationship with Hannah provides good insight into the Victorian caste-system. Hudson quotes profusely from this important source for the social historian in this somewhat repetitive and overlong biography.

(d) WORKING-CLASS MOVEMENTS [for religious influences, see 'The churches and social reform' in Section 7]

581. G. D. H. Cole, *A short history of the British working-class movement 1789–1947* (1948)

582. G. D. H. Cole and R. Postgate, *The common people, 1746–1946* (1938; 4th ed., 1949)

583. G. D. H. Cole and A. W. Filson (eds.), *British working-class movements: select documents, 1789–1875* (1951)

581 is a revised one-volume edition of a three-volume history published 1925–27. Like **582**, which covers similar ground, it was an exploratory study, which is still worth consulting and using alongside the selection of documents in **583**.

584. Z. Bauman, *Between class and elite. The evolution of the British labour movement: a sociological study* (1960; trans., 1972)

Originally published in Polish in 1960, this account of the gradual accommodation of the labour movement within the capitalist system lacks the sophistication of analysis that an awareness of recent research might have given it, and which is to be found, for example, in **586**.

585. J. L. and B. Hammond, *The age of the Chartists 1832–54. A study of discontent* (1930; repr. 1962)

Further 'pessimism' from the Hammonds, this time concerning the social conditions in which Chartism took root. Its conclusions have to be weighed against more recent research, but its spirit and structure (including novel chapters on drink, popular culture, and 'common enjoyment') make it a book still worth reading. *The bleak age* (1934; new ed., 1947) is a part of it, revised and reissued by the Hammonds.

586. T. R. Tholfsen, *Working-class radicalism in mid-Victorian England* (1976)

An anlysis of the 'acculturation' and 'deradicalisation' of the working-class movement in the twenty years after Chartism. The sub-culture which Tholfsen describes is very much that of working-class intellectuals and his book must therefore be read in the context of the debate about the labour aristocracy [see **181–82**] and the formation of class consciousness [see **577–78**].

587. J. T. Ward (ed.), *Popular movements c. 1830–50* (1970)

588. J. Stevenson and R. Quinault (eds.), *Popular protest and public order. Six studies in British history, 1790–1920* (1974)

587 is a collection of conventional essays on the most familiar movements, ranging in quality from a valuable chapter on Chartist histories to an indifferent one on public health. The essays on food riots and industrial disturbances in **588** are more specialised but a better indication of current preoccupations—indeed, they are the sort of limited research-projects that students might undertake.

589. D. Read, *Peterloo. The 'massacre' and its background* (1958)

590. R. Walmsley, *Peterloo: the case reopened* (1969)

591. J. Marlow, *The Peterloo massacre* (1969)

589 is the best short analysis of the massacre; **590** over-reacts in defending the government and the magistrates against E. P. Thompson's accusation that they deliberately forced the confrontation [see **559**]; and **591** is a popular account which adds nothing to the debate.

592. W. H. G. Armytage, *Heavens below: Utopian experiments in England, 1560–1960* (1961)

The fullest survey of millennial literature, but long in narrative and short in analysis.

593. G. D. H. Cole, *The life of Robert Owen* (1925; 3rd ed., 1965)

594. A. L. Morton, *The life and ideas of Robert Owen* (1962)

There are several biographies of Owen, from the detailed two-volume life by F. Podmore to the short, sound narrative by Margaret Cole. **593**, however, is the most balanced, and **594** is chiefly useful for the extracts from Owen's writings which it contains.

595. J. Butt (ed.), *Robert Owen, prince of cotton spinners* (1971)

596. S. Pollard and J. Salt (eds.), *Robert Owen: prophet of the poor. Essays in honour of the 200th anniversary of his birth* (1971)

These bicentenary essays are, on the whole, well-tempered tributes to the multi-faceted life of a 'prince' and a 'prophet'. [See also, Butt's essay in **506**.]

597. J. F. C. Harrison, *Robert Owen and the Owenites in Britain and America: the quest for the new moral world* (1969)

598. R. G. Garnett, *Cooperation and the Owenite socialist communities in Britain, 1825–45* (1972)

597 is by far the most penetrating study of Owenism as a body of ideas. It contains an exhaustive bibliography. Harrison's refreshing opinions on the communities seem to have been ignored in Garnett's turgid monograph on three of them.

599. M. Hovell, *The Chartist movement* (1918; 3rd ed., 1966)

600. J. T. Ward, *Chartism* (1973)

601. D. J. V. Jones, *Chartism and the Chartists* (1975)

602. A. Briggs (ed.), *Chartist studies* (1959)

603. F. C. Mather, *Chartism* (1965; 2nd ed., 1972)

604. D. Thompson (ed.), *The early Chartists* (1971)

There has been no shortage of histories of Chartism, from its economic and social characteristics to the reasons for its decline. [See the extensive new *Bibliography of the Chartist movement, 1837–1976* by J. F. C. Harrison and D. Thompson.] Despite the rich variety of such studies, however, a general historical survey for student purposes is still lacking, and one is obliged to fall back on Hovell's incomplete account of 1918. The two recent attempts at filling this gap have their shortcomings. **600** provides a basic narrative embodying the findings of much recent research, but it is at times over-compressed and offers little in the way of interpretation. By contrast, **601**'s thematic approach makes for excellent reading but only for someone with a grounding in the subject. The latter can be had from the short Historical Association pamphlet by F. C. Mather. A definitive history of Chartism will only be possible when its regional diversity is more fully understood, and much research is now being devoted towards this end, partly inspired by the ouststanding assemblage of essays in **602**. (Some idea of the ground still to be covered can be gauged from the fact that even this major collection of regional studies neglected two of the main centres of Chartist activity, namely London and Birmingham.) **604** is a serviceable anthology. [See also, **587, 588, 690, 828,** and **857–58.**]

605. G. D. H. Cole, *Chartist portraits* (1941; repr. 1965)

Chartist leaders too have not been neglected, and Cole's portrait-gallery of twelve of them is still the most useful introduction though it can be supplemented with excellent fuller biographies of John Frost, G. J. Harney, and Ernest Jones, and less satisfactory ones of the best known leaders, Feargus O'Connor and Bronterre O'Brien. [For the Chartist activities of Irish immigrants to the north of England, see Treble's essay in **506**.]

The Status of Women
[see also, **115–19** and **525–26**]

606. J. Dunbar, *The early Victorian woman. Some aspects of her life* [*1832–57*] (1953)

607. D. Crow, *The Victorian woman* (1971)

608. L. Davidoff, *The best circles: women and society in Victorian England* (1973)

606 is essentially a study of the social position of women (the 'aspects' are such things as marriage, home, shops, fashion and so on) and, despite the occasional genuflection to servants or women in industry or agriculture, it is a portrait of middle-class women that emerges. It lacks the political commitment, and hence the interest, of the more recent feminist literature. **607** is a far better introduction for the general reader to the variety of life-styles of Victorian women, and **608** is the most incisive of the three in its attempt to reconstruct patterns of behaviour, especially the rituals which were constructed by the 'best circles' to safeguard their status *vis à vis* the newly rich.

609. J. Kamm, *Rapiers and battleaxes. The woman's movement and its aftermath* (1966)

610. M. Ramelson, *The petticoat rebellion* (1967)

611. C. Rover, *Love, morals and the feminists* (1970)

612. S. Rowbotham, *Hidden from history: 300 years of women's oppression and the fight against it* (1973; 2nd ed., 1974)

The eruption of feminist studies in the past decade has not yet produced a satisfactory history of the woman's movement. **609** and **610** are dogmatic and disappointing and rely heavily on R. Strachey's history of 1928, and **611** is a slapdash treatment of an important theme. The best introduction is undoubtedly **612**, but even this is better on the political than on the social emancipation of women, and a comprehensive social history of women in the pre-suffragette period remains to be written.

613. M. Vicinus (ed.), *Suffer and be still: women in the Victorian age* (1972)

The high quality of the articles reprinted in this book does, however, augur well for the future of women's studies, though some of its subjects—such as Victorian women and menstruation—are rather too recondite for premature perusal. But its impeccable bibliographical article does merit early consideration.

614. W. F. Neff, *Victorian working women. An historical and literary study of women in British industries and professions 1832–50* (1929; repr. 1966)

615. P. Branca, *Silent sisterhood. Middle-class women in the Victorian home* (1975)

616. I. Pinchbeck, *Women workers and the industrial revolution, 1750–1850* (1930; repr. 1969)

617. M. Hewitt, *Wives and mothers in Victorian industry* (1958)

618. L. Holcombe, *Victorian ladies at work: middle-class working women in England and Wales, 1850–1914* (1973)

614 draws upon historical and literary evidence to portray the working lives of women in the early Victorian period. It includes also a chapter on 'idle' women, a theme developed more fully in **615**'s analysis of the domestic life of middle-class women, a serious attempt to destroy the stereotyped image which characterises even some of the most perceptive historical literature. **616** is still the best account of the changing status of women in agriculture and industry during the upheavals of industrialisation. The title of **617** is rather misleading for its theme is the effects of industrialisation on home life, focusing in particular on female cotton operatives. And, lastly, **618** looks at five occupations open to middle-class women in the late nineteenth century and, though a rather dull book, contains an informative body of facts and statistics.

Children

619. M. C. Lochhead, *Their first ten years: Victorian childhood* (1956)

620. M. C. Lochhead, *Young Victorians* (1959)

621. I. Pinchbeck and M. Hewitt, *Children in English society. Vol. ii: From the eighteenth century to the Children Act 1948* (1973)

Social

622. P. Horn, *The Victorian country child* (1974)

623. M. V. Hughes, *A London child of the 1870s* (1934; repr. 1977)

Most writing on the place of children in society was of the pleasant lazy-Sunday-afternoon type represented by Lochhead's two volumes. Our ignorance is now in the process of being banished thanks to the three ladies who have amassed the information presented in **621** and **622**. Molly Hughes's account of her own childhood provides an urban counterpart to Flora Thompson's rural upbringing [**548**] and a middle-class contrast to the poverty of Roberts's Salford childhood [**702**].

Sexuality

624. R. Pearsall, *The worm in the bud: the world of Victorian sexuality* (1969)

625. R. Pearsall, *Public purity, private shame. Victorian sexual hypocrisy exposed* (1976)

Scandal in history has the same vicarious attraction for its readers as the *exposés* of the Sunday newspapers, and unfortunately most historical writing on the subject has been of a similar sensational ilk. But sex sells books and so we are likely to continue to be confronted with anecdotal and titillating rubbish of this type.

626. S. Marcus, *The other Victorians: a study of sexuality and pornography in mid-nineteenth-century England* (1964)

627. E. Trudgill, *Madonnas and Magdalens: the origins and development of Victorian sexual attitudes* (1976)

Two serious but patchy attempts at examining Victorian sexuality. The evidence of the first rests on too slender a base, most notably the sexual adventures of the insatiable author of *My secret life* (available, incidentally, in a three-volume edition) and the activities of a bibliographer of pornography. The second is a limited but praiseworthy exploration of the attitudes of the sexes towards each other.

628. C. Terrot, *The maiden tribute. A study of the white slave traffic of the nineteenth century* (1959)

629. M. Pearson, *The age of consent. Victorian prostitution and its enemies* (1972)

Novelistic and popular accounts of prostitution and the traffic in young virgins. **629** uses the same main title and covers much the same ground as, but makes no reference to, a book written by A. Stafford and published in 1964. The subject cries out for a serious sociological analysis. [See, however, E. M. Sigsworth and T. J. Wyke's essay in **613**, and E. Trudgill's essay in **706**.]

Leisure

630. R. W. Malcolmson, *Popular recreations in English society 1700–1850* (1973)

631. S. Margetson, *Leisure and pleasure in the nineteenth century* (1969)

632. H. E. Meller, *Leisure and the changing city, 1870–1914* (1976)

Our own leisured age is only just beginning to examine the pastimes (other than those in the previous section!) of earlier periods. **630** is solid on the recreations of a pre-industrial society but stops short of explaining how certain 'sports' (such as cock-fighting) were taken over by the city, or reshaped into their modern form (such as football), or, indeed, why certain pastimes survived industrialisation (such as the wakes). **631** explains why opportunities for leisure-activities increased in the course of the nineteenth century, but is generally too descriptive. The 'changing city' of **632** is Bristol, and the study is a narrow one which barely touches upon certain important social pleasures such as drinking or music-hall entertainment. Indeed, the best account of the former is to be found in **694**, and of the latter in **943**.

633. A. Delgado, *Victorian entertainment* (1971)

634. J. A. R. Pimlott, *The Englishman's holiday. A social history* (1947; repr. 1976)

633 is a light and well-illustrated treatment of its subject; **634** is a diverting account of the roots of a modern industry. Certain leisure-pastimes such as football and horse-racing have recently been moved out of the realm of the anecdotal and into that of serious historical investigation, which augurs well for a future general study. Delgado has also recently examined the growth in popularity of the annual outing.

Social Reform

(a) GENERAL

635. E. C. Midwinter, *Victorian social reform* (1968)

A short introduction and guide to further reading in the 'Seminar studies' series [see **70**].

636. M. Bruce, *The coming of the welfare state* (1961)

637. D. Fraser, *The evolution of the British welfare state: a history of social policy since the industrial revolution* (1973)

638. D. Roberts, *Victorian origins of the British welfare state* (1960)

639. M. Bruce (ed.), *The rise of the welfare state: English social policy, 1601–1971* (1973)

640. R. C. Birch, *The shaping of the welfare state* (1974)

636 and **637** are surveys of the origins and development of the welfare state, the latter being marginally the better on the nineteenth century, though both neglect the study of ideas and attitudes for a political emphasis. **638** is a more specialised discussion of administrative growth and the motives behind state intervention and should be read in conjunction with other books that examine this issue [see **82–91**]. The bulk of the documents in **639** are drawn from the nineteenth and twentieth centuries and complement the text of **636**. **640** is one of the 'Seminar studies' [see **70**].

641. B. B. Gilbert, *The evolution of national insurance in Great Britain: the origins of the welfare state* (1966)

642. J. Harris, *Unemployment and politics: a study in English social policy 1886–1914* (1972)

643. J. R. Hay, *The origins of the Liberal welfare reforms 1906–14* (1975)

The reforms of the pre-war Liberal government figure prominently in these three books. Although Gilbert's story concerns national insurance it does bring out well the broader change in attitudes which paved the way for collectivist legislation. Likewise, Harris's careful unravelling of the unemployment saga demonstrates how and why a hitherto mainly parochial concern became a predominantly national one. Hay's pamphlet belongs to the 'Studies in economic and social history' series [see **82**].

644. D. Owen, *English philanthropy, 1660–1960* (1965)

645. C. L. Mowat, *The Charity Organisation Society, 1869–1913* (1961)

646. K. Woodroofe, *From charity to social work in England and the United States* (1962)

647. A. F. Young and E. T. Ashton, *British social work in the nineteenth century* (1956)

Charitable activities and the attitudes and aims of social workers are well-surveyed in these four books. Their titles indicate clearly their different emphases. [See also **785–87.**]

648. M. B. Simey, *Charitable effort in Liverpool in the nineteenth century* (1951)

649. E. C. Midwinter, *Social administration in Lancashire, 1830–60: Poor Law, public health and police* (1969)

Local social work has not received the attention from historians which it merits, and these two studies—the one of voluntary, the other of official activities—are therefore doubly valuable.

650. H. W. Pfautz (ed.), *Charles Booth on the city. Physical pattern and social structure: selected writings* (1967)

651. A. Fried and R. M. Elman (eds.), *Charles Booth's London. A portrait of the poor at the turn of the century, drawn from his 'Life and labour of the people in London'* (1967)

652. D. C. Jones, *Social surveys* (1949)

653. P. J. Keating (ed.), *Into unknown England, 1866–1913* (1976)

The social historian's debt to the work of Booth and Rowntree is immeasurable. Their methods can be studied in the accounts by their biographers (especially Asa Briggs on Rowntree and T. S. and M. B. Simey on Booth) and more briefly in **652**. But none of these is a substitute for their own writings, and Booth's mammoth seventeen-volume *Life and labour of the people in London* (1889–1903) can be sampled through the selections of extracts in **650** and **651**. But Rowntree's *Poverty* (1901) is not easily available and should be reprinted. Keating's anthology is drawn from a much wider range of social investigators, some of them obscure, though less so once one has read his illuminating introduction. M. J. Cullen has also thrown interesting light on the investigative work of the early Victorian statistical societies.

(b) POVERTY AND THE POOR LAW

654. W. H. Chaloner, *The hungry forties* (1957)

655. A. Seldon (ed.), *The long debate on poverty* (1972)

656. A. J. Taylor (ed.), *The standard of living in Britain in the industrial revolution* (1975)

The extent to which working-class living standards rose or fell in the early decades of the nineteenth century has been hotly debated by historians, mainly in the journals. Some of their articles have, however, been reprinted in books already mentioned [see, for example, **181** and **396**], but the principal ones are reproduced in **656**. The essays included in **655**, however, commissioned from right-wing historians by the Institute of Economic Affairs, are hardly calculated to give a balanced view of the debate. The present author shares E. P. Thompson's opinion [see **559**] that while living standards may have risen according to quantifiable criteria (real wages, etc.), the quality of life certainly deteriorated. However, a final judgement will not be possible until more local studies have been undertaken, and probably not even then if the distinction between what is measurable and what is not is accepted. **654**, an Historical Association pamphlet, is a short assessment of the degree of poverty in one decade by an 'optimist'. However, it is only peripheral to the standard-of-living debate as few historians now think of the 1840s, at least after 1842, as meriting the sobriquet 'the hungry decade' which was so long attached to it. Some of the recent work done on diet by, amongst others, J. Burnett, D. J. Oddy and D. S. Miller, has cast new light on living standards, particularly in the period after 1850.

657. B. Rodgers, *The battle against poverty. Vol. i: From pauperism to human rights* (1968)

A beginner's guide to the Poor Law system of the nineteenth century. The fullest description is still that of Sidney and Beatrice Webb to be found in volumes seven to nine (*English Poor Law history*) of their classic *English local government* [see **299**].

658. J. D. Marshall, *The old Poor Law, 1795–1834* (1968)

659. J. R. Poynter, *Society and pauperism: English ideas on poor relief, 1795–1834* (1968)

660. B. Inglis, *Poverty and the industrial revolution* (1971)

661. M. I. Thomis, *Responses to industrialisation. The British experience 1780–1850* (1976)

658 is a review of historical scholarship on Speenhamland and other aspects of the old Poor Law in the 'Studies in economic and social history' series [see **82**]. **659** is a thoroughly researched and thoughtful account of contemporary ideas on the problem of pauperism, better balanced on the whole than **660** which is concerned more particularly with the few 'men of conscience' who sought to ameliorate the social hardships created by the industrial revolution. And **661** is an attempt to assess just how far Britons were in fact even aware of the 'revolutionary' economic and social changes of the age through which they were living.

662. M. E. Rose, *The relief of poverty 1834–1914* (1972)

663. D. Fraser (ed.), *The new Poor Law in the nineteenth century* (1976)

Rose's pamphlet in the 'Studies in economic and social history' series [see **82**] takes the discussion in **658** down into the later nineteenth century and the era of the new Poor Law. Much of the debate concerning poor relief has been conducted in the historical journals and so these two pamphlets are particularly estimable as guides to that material. The eight essays in **663** are concerned, as the blurb on the cover of the book puts it, with 'five cardinal aspects of poor relief' (settlement, medical treatment, education, philanthropy, and politics) and the operation of the Poor Law in 'three contrasting geographical dimensions: in towns, and in the countryside (in England and Wales), and generally in Scotland'. As is often the case the contents are rather more mundane than the publisher's advertisement suggests, but on the whole the collection is a valuable one with fine pieces by Rose, Flinn, and McCord, a good introduction by Fraser which links the essays together, and a helpful bibliographical guide at the end. [See also, Blaug's essay in **505**.]

664. M. E. Rose (ed.), *The English Poor Law 1780–1930* (1971)

Documents with short comments and an introduction by the editor—in the same series as **738**.

665. N. C. Edsall, *The Anti-Poor Law movement, 1833–44* (1971)

As one of the few monographs on political opposition to the new Poor Law this is disappointing for it neglects many important questions suggested by its title, while the usual information about administration and enforcement of the law intrudes to a large and unwarranted degree. [Rose's essay in **587** is shorter but better.]

666. R. G. Hodgkinson, *The origins of the National Health Service. The medical services of the new Poor Law, 1834–71* (1967)

A long-winded and not very convincing attempt to show that in the gradual triumph of the humane medical aspects of poor relief over its harsh deterrent side lay the foundations of the welfare state. However, the book is a mine of information on the Poor Law medical services. [Cf. **638** and **641**.]

667. N. Longmate, *The workhouse* (1974)

It is surprising that in their enthusiasm for debating the administrative aspects of poor relief, historians have relegated to a minor place an inquiry into workhouse conditions. These Longmate vividly describes, though it is clear that more local studies are necessary before any generalisations can be confidently made.

668. S. G. and E. O. A. Checkland (eds.), *The Poor Law report of 1834* (1974)

A paperback edition, nicely introduced and produced, for those who wish to consult the report upon which the legislation of 1834 was based.

(c) FACTORY LEGISLATION

669. B. L. Hutchins and A. Harrison, *A history of factory legislation* (1903; 3rd ed., 1926)

Remains the best general account.

670. M. W. Thomas, *The early factory legislation. A study in legislative and administrative evolution* (1948)

671. U. Henriques, *The early Factory Acts and their enforcement* (1974)

The short Historical Association pamphlet by Henriques is far easier to digest than Thomas's detailed consideration of legislation in the first half of the nineteenth century.

672. J. T. Ward, *The factory movement, 1830–55* (1962)

The familiar details of factory legislation and the lives of reformers such as Shaftesbury have been integrated to produce a rounded account of the factory movement. [See also, his shorter essay on the same subject in **587**.]

673. J. T. Ward, *The factory system. Vol. i: Birth and growth* (1970)

A collection of documents in the less than satisfactory 'Sources for social and economic history' series [see **738**].

(d) PUBLIC HEALTH [see also, **587**]

674. W. M. Frazer, *A history of English public health, 1834–1939* (1950)

675. C. F. Brockington, *A short history of public health* (1956; 2nd ed., 1966)

676. M. W. Flinn, *Public health reform in Britain* (1968)

674 is standard if somewhat factual. The title of **675** is a little misleading in that while it summarises public health history it also concentrates on a number of special aspects such as neglected children, mental health, and venereal disease. A good short introduction to the subject is **676** which contains an appendix of documents, though the best introduction of all is an Open University course-unit by R. Hodgkinson, entitled *Science and public health*. Flinn has also edited Chadwick's seminal *Report on the sanitary condition of the labouring population of Great Britain (1842)*.

677. R. A. Lewis, *Edwin Chadwick and the public health movement, 1832–54* (1952)

678. S. E. Finer, *The life and times of Sir Edwin Chadwick* (1952)

679. R. Lambert, *Sir John Simon, 1816–1904, and English social administration* (1963)

678 is an excellent full-length biography though in certain respects it is surpassed for the important phase of the public health movement by **677**'s fine study. Simon has also found his apotheosis in Lambert's biography. These brilliant studies of two of the age's greatest social administrators convey a more up-to-date, more thoroughly-researched, and certainly more interesting picture of nineteenth-century public health than is available in any of the general surveys.

680. N. Longmate, *King Cholera. The biography of a disease* (1966)

681. R. J. Morris, *Cholera 1832* (1976)

Those who have read *Bleak House* will have some inkling of the social importance of cholera and the awe in which it was held by the Victorians. **680** is a popular and **681** a serious study of the scourge and attempts to combat it. Historians have recently begun to turn their attention to the social history of medicine, and this is proving a valuable contribution to our understanding of public health and the treatment of disease.

(e) ANTI-SLAVERY

682. E. E. Williams, *Capitalism and slavery* (1944)

683. H. Temperley, *British anti-slavery, 1833–70* (1972)

684. E. F. Hurwitz, *Politics and the public conscience. Slave emancipation and the Abolitionist Movement in Britain* (1973)

Temperley's monograph is now the standard treatment of its

subject, though Williams's more provocative argument that slavery was abolished because it ceased to be economically viable deserves serious consideration. By contrast, the strictly conventional approach of Hurwitz's book, half of which is a collection of documents, is set by its first sentence: 'The success of the British Anti-Slavery Movement indicates that there have been moments in British history when values have taken precedence over economics, when the spiritual triumphed over the material.' Temperley summarises some of his findings in his contribution to **55**.

(f) CRIME AND PUNISHMENT

685. J. J. Tobias, *Crime and industrial society in the nineteenth century* (1967)

686. J. J. Tobias, *Nineteenth-century crime: prevention and punishment* (1972)

687. K. Chesney, *The Victorian underworld* (1970)

688. R. D. Altick, *Victorian studies in scarlet* (1972)

It is surprising in view of the inveteracy of crime, that there have been so few sociological studies of the impact of industrialisation on the criminal community and on the type, treatment, and punishment of crime. Part of the difficulty lies in the inadequacy of criminal statistics for the early part of the century [see the essay by Gattrell and Hadden in **524**], but Tobias has made a useful and informative beginning, and **686** serves as a commentary on the documents in **687** which, like the rest of the series to which it belongs [see **738**], is deficient in this respect. Chesney's study of the underworld will, however, seem original only to those who have not read Mayhew to whom he is so patently indebted (though he does not acknowledge the fact). Most studies of criminal behaviour have been popular narratives of the type represented here by **688**, a very readable but not very enlightening account of famous murders.

689. T. A. Critchley, *A history of police in England and Wales 900–1966* (1967)

690. F. C. Mather, *Public order in the age of the Chartists* (1959)

689 (inevitably published in Great Britain by Constable!), is the standard survey of police history. Its narrative is, however, flat and uninspired, and lacks the sort of insights that Mather brings to his inquiry into the problems of maintaining public order in the early nineteenth century. There is also a short and instructive pamphlet by E. C. Midwinter on law and order in early Victorian Lancashire.

691. A. Harding, *A social history of English law* (1966)

692. L. Radzinowicz, *A history of English criminal law and its administration from 1750* (4 vols., 1948–68)

There are many detailed legal histories as well as biographies of eminent practitioners, but they seldom find a place on a general history degree course. The hare started by Harding in his survey of the relation of legal developments to social history has unfortunately not been pursued by a closer look at this theme in its nineteenth-century context. **692** is the fullest and most comprehensive of the histories of criminal law. Volume one is primarily concerned with punishment, particularly of capital offenders, and with the reform of criminal law; volume two with prevention and deterrence; volume three with police reform; and volume four takes up again the story of the reform of the capital laws and the establishment of a regular police force. R. S. E. Hinde's old account of the British penal system still merits occasional consideration.

693. H. Mayhew and J. Binny, *The criminal prisons of London and scenes of prison life* (1862; repr. 1971)

Lengthy but contains passages of vintage Mayhew. [See also, **299**.]

(g) TEMPERANCE [see also, **299**]

694. B. Harrison, *Drink and the Victorians: the temperance question in England, 1815–72* (1971)

695. N. Longmate, *The waterdrinkers. A history of temperance* (1968)

694 is a magnificent study of temperance and many other aspects of the drink question which makes the popular account by Longmate appear by comparison slight and trivial. One quotation from it will serve to illustrate its bold and arresting style: '. . . the railway', Harrison writes, 'probably did more for temperance in the nineteenth century—the gaslamp more for morality—than either the temperance movement or the Vice Society.' All-in-all, it is a book as refreshing as its subject. Harrison, too, has produced the best social history of the public house in his contribution to **706**, though there are several books on the subject, some of them, such as that by M. Girouard, are exceptionally well-illustrated.

(h) HOUSING

696. D. Rubinstein, *Victorian homes* (1974)

A collection of nearly two hundred extracts from contemporary accounts of various aspects of nineteenth-century home life (architecture, sanitation, general living conditions, and so on) at all levels of society. Rubinstein's brief commentary and, more particularly, his guide to further reading, make this a useful starting-point in the absence of a general history of housing.

697. J. N. Tarn, *Working-class housing in nineteenth-century Britain* (1971)

698. J. N. Tarn, *Five per cent philanthropy: an account of housing in urban areas between 1840 and 1914* (1974)

699. E. Gauldie, *Cruel habitations. A history of working-class housing 1780–1918* (1974)

700. S. D. Chapman (ed.), *The history of working-class housing: a symposium* (1971)

Tarn and Gauldie have pioneered studies of working-class housing conditions, reform proposals, and housing legislation. They could both have profited by more local studies of the quality of those included in **700**.

701. R. Roberts, *The classic slum. Salford life in the first quarter of the century* (1971)

702. R. Roberts, *A ragged schooling. Growing up in the classic slum* (1976)

Although not specifically housing histories, these two books (the first a piece of social history, the second a fragment of autobiography) shed light through Roberts's colourful eye for detail on many aspects of slum life.

Urban History
[see also, 'Local government' in Section 2, 'Urban society' in this section, and **123** and **197**]

(a) GENERAL

703. H. J. Dyos (ed.), *The study of urban history* (1968)

704. A. Everitt (ed.), *Perspectives in English urban history* (1973)

Some of the general papers in **703**, such as that by S. G. Checkland, provide the best introduction to this relatively new branch of historical inquiry. These two books also contain a number of essays on more specialised aspects of urban development. Those by Foster, Newton, and Hennock have since been developed by their authors at greater length elsewhere. [See **303** and **577**.]

705. A. Briggs, *Victorian cities* (1963)

Excellent chapters on Manchester, Leeds, Birmingham, Middlesbrough, London, and Melbourne—a 'Victorian community overseas'—with an introduction and conclusion which highlight both the similarities and the uniqueness of the cities studied.

706. H. J. Dyos and M. Wolff (eds.), *The Victorian city: images and realities* (2 vols., 1973; repr. 4 vols., 1976–)

The upsurge in interest in the history of the city in the 1960s made possible the symposium on the subject organised by *Victorian Studies* in 1967 and the resultant publication of this magisterial collection of thirty-eight papers ranging over many aspects of urban life, and backed up by over 400 excellent photographs and illustrations. The price of the hardback edition unfortunately placed it beyond the reach of all but libraries and wealthy professors, but it is now thankfully in the process of being reissued in a four-volume paperback edition which has trimmed the price but not the quality.

707. W. Ashworth, *The genesis of modern British town planning. A study in economic and social history of the nineteenth and twentieth centuries* (1954)

708. J. R. Kellett, *The impact of railways on Victorian cities* (1969)

709. B. I. Coleman (ed.), *The idea of the city in nineteenth-century Britain* (1973)

Three innovatory studies of particular aspects of urban development. **707** provides, as its author intended, a preliminary survey of the growth of town planning and one which, in the light of the mushrooming of urban studies, deserves a successor; **708** asks how the railways affected the five largest conurbations in terms of social cost; and the collection of documents edited by Coleman for the 'Birth of modern Britain' series [see **576**] demonstrates the way contemporaries viewed the change from a rural to a predominantly urban landscape. In connection with this last viewpoint, the 'literary' response to the city (and the country) and its frequent divorce from social reality is the subject of a book by Raymond Williams.

(b) A NOTE ON BOOKS ON PARTICULAR TOWNS

710. H. J. Dyos, *Victorian suburb: a study of the growth of Camberwell* (1961)

The Victorians were as prone to marking their triumphs in urban developments as much with monumental histories as with monumental town-halls. But while the latter have largely survived and are familiar to us all the former appear antiquarian and have been generally ignored by posterity. The more scientific approach of recent historians has led to the replacement of these older studies by critical and penetrating modern appraisals. Their number is growing all the time but as yet they do not figure prominently on undergraduate reading-lists (except where the history of a particular city appears on the local history course of its university or students opt for a specialised course in urban history). One of the best examples of this type of case-study is Dyos's history of Camberwell which, in addition to fulfilling its stated purpose, no doubt parallels the experiences of other districts enveloped by the urban sprawl. There are, for example, modern histories of London (the recent account by D. J. Olsen is the best) and of several of its suburbs, of Ashton-under-Lyne, Birmingham, Crewe, Nottingham, Lincoln, Exeter, York, Leicester, Wantage, Gateshead, West Hartlepool, Southampton, Liverpool, St Helens, Grimsby, Newcastle-upon-Tyne, Middlesbrough, and Sheffield. The city which cries out for a new history is Manchester [but see, **561**], though many important industrial towns, such as Bradford, also require new treatment.

(c) PHOTOGRAPHIC COLLECTIONS

Collections of photographs are a growth area in publishing. They can conjure up reality for many students far more readily than the written word, which requires an imaginative response. Even those which fall into the category of coffee-table books are usually of some use in teaching. The inclusion of photographs in history books seem to have become almost a statutory obligation. They often appear to be for light relief or glossiness rather than to serve a serious purpose since the descriptions which accompany them are so inadequate as to be all but worthless. It would be impossible in a bibliography of this sort even to attempt to review all this material. The interested reader should turn to the essay by G. H. Martin and D. Francis, 'The camera's eye', in **706**; 'Authenticity and charm: the revival of Victorian photography' by Alan Thomas which appeared in *Victorian Studies*, XVIII (September, 1974); and H. and A. Gernsheim, *A concise history* *of photography* (1965) which is a good, general introduction to the subject. Photography has therefore been a boon to the social historian, and, perhaps above all, since landscapes constantly change, to the urban historian. In this connection, it is worth singling out one very extensive series published by Batsford and entitled 'The past in photographs', though they are not alone in the field (see, for example, the catalogues of David & Charles and Gordon Fraser). The urban historian also relies on nineteenth-century ordnance survey maps, especially the large-scale town maps, and a good introduction to their use is J. B. Harley and C. W. Phillips's, *The historian's guide to ordnance survey maps* (1964).

6
EDUCATION

The history of education is properly a major branch of social history. But it merits a separate section in this bibliography partly because it forms a significant part of courses foisted upon hapless trainee teachers by those who regard a knowledge of educational history as somehow critical to teaching-ability; and, more seriously, because until recently much writing on the subject was not in fact social history but a dreary (and oft-repeated) narrative of administrative history concerned with voluntary organisations, government legislation, and so on. Institutional history of this sort is now thankfully being superseded by studies which consider just what it was like to have been at the receiving end of this educational process, and has been assisted by a correspondingly new interest in the history of children [see **619-23**]. The selection that follows has tried to do justice to this trend by emphasising those books that form part of it as well as by ignoring many of the conventional, and narrower, administrative histories. I have therefore excluded with few qualms monographs on the school inspectorate, on the role of particular churches in educational provision, on the origins of the Department of Education and Science, on classical education, and on the growth of a public examination system. I have with greater regret not been able to review the local studies which are now beginning to appear (for example, of village schools in Devon and Derbyshire, a church school in Kensington, educational provision in Nottingham and Liverpool and school attendance in London) and which should eventually permit a more vital reconstruction. Nor have I been able to find space for specialised monographs on girls' education, the Working Men's College, individual colleges and universities (and, particularly, the political influence of Victorian Oxford and Cambridge along with the careers of some of their dons—notably Pattison, Jowett, and Vaughan), or, indeed, the several extant biographies of educationalists.

General

(a) HISTORY

711. W. H. G. Armytage, *Four hundred years of English education* (1964)

712. H. C. Barnard, *A history of English education from 1760* (1961)

713. S. J. Curtis, *History of education in Great Britain* (1948; 7th ed., 1967)

Three conventional general outlines with little to choose between them. **713** is a marginally better primer, mainly because of its section on Scottish developments.

714. J. W. Adamson, *English education, 1789–1902* (1930; repr. 1965)

715. S. J. Curtis and M. E. A. Boultwood, *An introductory history of English education since 1800* (1960; 4th ed., 1966)

716. I. Morrish, *Education since 1800* (1970)

714 has been for nearly half a century the standard introduction to all aspects of nineteenth-century English education. **715** is a flat narrative and **716** a very broad outline with a bibliographical guide at the end of each chapter.

717. J. Lawson and H. Silver, *A social history of education in England* (1973)

718. P. W. Musgrave, *Society and education in England since 1800* (1968)

Despite the promise of their titles both of these books are a little disappointing, the first because it is still essentially traditional 'institutional' history, the second because it fails to fulfil satisfactorily its stated purpose of showing 'the changing interrelationships of education with such other social institutions as the family, the economy, or the social class system'.

719. J. S. Maclure (ed.), *Educational documents. England and Wales 1816–1967* (1965; 2nd ed., 1967)

720. E. E. Cowie, *Education* (1973)

721. P. H. J. H. Gosden, *How they were taught. An anthology of contemporary accounts of learning and teaching in England 1800–1950* (1969)

Education

722. A. E. Dyson and J. Lovelock (eds.), *Education and democracy* (1975)

Four very different compilations of documents. **719** is drawn primarily from the blue books with the aim of showing 'the slow and often tortuous process by which a public system of education has been built'. It is inevitably rather dry. **720** is one of the documentary-cum-text volumes in the series 'Examining the evidence' [see **307**]. **721** is a much more interesting selection of contemporary opinions on education. Each document is given a concise contextual explanation and the whole is well-illustrated by its thirty-two plates. But the most stimulating collection of all is **722** in the 'Birth of modern Britain' series [see **576**]. Its extracts are chosen from prominent literary and political figures of the nineteenth century and illustrate the extent to which education, in an era of advancing democracy, was used to reaffirm the existing social hierarchy.

(b) THEORY

723. S. J. Curtis and M. E. A. Boultwood, *A short history of educational ideas* (1953; 4th ed., 1965)

Wide-ranging but contains two chapters on English educational writers of the nineteenth century which provide a short introduction to the subject.

724. H. M. Pollard, *Pioneers of popular education 1760–1850* (1956)

725. W. A. C. Stewart and W. P. McCann, *The educational innovators. Vol. i: 1750–1880; Vol. ii* (by W. A. C. Stewart): *Progressive schools 1881–1967* (1967–68)

The selection of British pioneers in the second part of **724** is unbalanced in its consideration of some minor, to the exclusion of a few major, figures. By contrast, **725** is a work of painstaking scholarship which concentrates on those educationalists who sought fundamental change, rather than mere modification, of established methods.

726. H. Silver, *The concept of popular education. A study of ideas and social movements in the early nineteenth century* (1965)

727. H. Silver, *English education and the radicals 1780–1850* (1975)

Silver's later book makes an interesting contrast between the attempts of middle- and working-class radicals to use education as a vehicle of social change, though it repeats arguments (particularly concerning Owenism) used in the earlier book—arguments which even in 1965 were not altogether original.

728. R. G. McPherson, *The theory of higher education in nineteenth-century England* (1959)

Mainly a summary of the ideas of half-a-dozen theorists which therefore does not fulfil the grander claim of its title.

Elementary and Secondary

729. E. C. Midwinter, *Nineteenth-century education* (1970)

730. G. Sutherland, *Elementary education in the nineteenth century* (1971)

Two short introductions, the first a volume in the 'Seminar studies' series [see **70**], the second an Historical Association pamphlet.

731. M. Sturt, *The education of the people. A history of primary education in England and Wales in the nineteenth century* (1967)

732. D. Wardle, *English popular education 1780–1975* (1970; 2nd ed., 1976)

733. N. Middleton and S. Weitzmann, *A place for everyone. A history of state education from the eighteenth century to the 1970s* (1976)

731 is well-written and throws new light on the content of the primary syllabus. **732** indicates the deficiencies at the present time in our knowledge of the history of education and suggests themes that might form the basis of a theoretical study, though it is unfortunately confined to raising questions rather than answering them. **733** is an indictment of the state's perpetuation of an elitist system of education and its failure to develop a science-orientated curriculum.

734. B. Simon, *Studies in the history of education, 1780–1870* (1960)

735. B. Simon, *Education and the labour movement, 1870–1920* (1965)

736. J. M. Goldstrom, *The social content of education, 1808–70; a study of the working-class school reader in England and Ireland* (1972)

737. E. G. West, *Education and the industrial revolution* (1975)

Four stimulating studies which stand out in a sea of banality. Simon's two volumes marked a major departure from conventional outlines by looking at the provision of education from below, that is from the point of view of the working classes, rather than from above, that is from the point of view of government and institutions. Goldstrom takes this development further by examining the content of what was taught and assessing its influence on the 'consumers', the children themselves. He concludes that despite the sectarian wrangling which dominated the debate on education, the precepts imparted by the different schools were in essence the same. By contrast, West's book is worth reading for its development historically of the heterodox argument which originally appeared in his *Education and the state* that educational progress was being made regardless of state intervention and that the latter may even have hindered it.

738. J. M. Goldstrom (ed.), *Education: elementary education 1780–1900* (1972)

A collection of documents in David & Charles's series 'Sources for social and economic history' (distributed in North America by Barnes & Noble), the aim of which is 'to let the original authorities speak for themselves—as a basis for discussion and essay writing in sixth forms, colleges and universities . . .'. The volumes in this particular series seem to be, more than is usually the case, cobbled together with little serious instructive commentary; in other words, to be the product of the publishing sausage-machine.

739. J. Murphy, *Church, state and schools in Britain, 1800–1970* (1971)

740. J. Hurt, *Education in evolution: church, state, society and popular education, 1800–70* (1971)

Murphy, the author of an important study of the religious problem in educational provision in Liverpool, has written the best short introduction to the relationship between religion and education. Hurt's revaluation of the quality of sectarian education prior to 1870 anticipated some of the arguments of **737**.

741. E. E. Rich, *The Education Act of 1870* (1970)

742. J. Murphy, *The Education Act 1870: text and commentary* (1972)

741 is not specifically a study of the 1870 act but a collection of competent essays on nineteenth-century elementary education. **742** *is* what its title claims to be, and Murphy, as one might expect (see comment on **739**), writes particularly well on the religious background to the act.

743. G. Sutherland, *Policy-making in elementary education 1870–95* (1973)

Uses educational administration to test the theories of MacDonagh and Parris [see **85**] concerning government growth. [Cf. **829**.]

744. G. A. N. Lowndes, *The silent social revolution. An account of the expansion of public education in England and Wales 1895–1965* (1937; 2nd ed., 1969)

745. E. J. R. Eaglesham, *The foundations of twentieth-century education in England* (1967)

The bulk of **744** is concerned with the post-1902 period, but it provides a brief, if somewhat conventional, account of the school board era and the background to the 1902 Education Act. **745** is a thought-provoking essay on the problems confronting elementary education in the last decade of the nineteenth century, and an assessment of the legislation of 1902, particularly the role played in its construction by Robert Morant and the Board of Education.

746. A. M. Kazamias, *Politics, society and secondary education in England* (1966)

747. R. L. Archer, *Secondary education in the nineteenth century* (1921; repr. 1966)

Two straightforward conventional accounts of the development of secondary education, the first confining itself to public secondary education from the time of the Bryce Commission report of 1895, the second dealing with all aspects of secondary education—private, state, university and the activities of the Misses Beale and Buss in the realm of girls' education.

Public Schools

748. T. W. Bamford, *The rise of the public schools. A study of boys' public boarding schools in England and Wales from 1837 to the present day* (1967)

749. V. Ogilvie, *The English public school* (1957)

There are a number of monographs on the major public (i.e. private) schools, but Bamford's book is the best general account of their history from the time of Victoria's accession onwards. It is particularly good on Rugby, as befits the author of the standard biography of Thomas Arnold. Ogilvie's has a much broader perspective, tracing the history of the schools since the Middle Ages, and as such has much less to say on the nineteenth century.

750. D. Newsome, *Godliness and good learning: four studies on a Victorian ideal* (1961)

751. A. C. Percival, *Very superior men. Some early public school headmasters and their achievements* (1973)

The four studies of **750** are of three headmasters (Thomas Arnold, J. P. Lee and E. W. Benson) and of the transition from 'godliness' to 'manliness' as the *leitmotiv* of public school education. **751** includes still more pen-portraits, with the ubiquitous Thomas Arnold again figuring prominently among them. Together these two books provide perceptive biographical details on the men who shaped the public schools.

752. R. Wilkinson, *The prefects: British leadership and the public school tradition* (1964)

An attempt to equate public school education with the training of a governing elite—an important theme which deserves better handling than it receives here.

Universities

753. V. H. H. Green, *The universities* (1969)

754. W. H. G. Armytage, *Civic universities. Aspects of a British tradition* (1955)

755. M. Sanderson (ed.), *The universities in the nineteenth century* (1975)

There is still room for a general study of the universities in the nineteenth century along the lines touched upon briefly in Sanderson's preface and introduction to his collection of documents in the 'Birth of modern Britain' series [see **576**]. For the moment, **753** is the best short survey providing a basic outline history in its first part (including a chapter on the Scottish universities) and a consideration of particular topics (such as the universities and science, or politics, or religion) in the second. The contents of **754** are too general to offer much more than an introduction to the nineteenth-century history of the civic universities—the period, in Armytage's terminology, of their 'efflorescence'.

756. M. Sanderson, *The universities and British industry, 1850–1970* (1972)

The most detailed account to date of the universities' response to rapid developments in the natural sciences, engineering and the social sciences, particularly apposite in Britain to the recent bout of soul-searching of the so-called educational 'great debate'.

757. J. H. (Cardinal) Newman, *The idea of a university* (1853 and 1858; 1 vol. ed., 1873; numerous subsequent editions, the most recent, 1976)

Originally published in two parts in the 1850s, this was undoubtedly the most important treatise on university education which appeared in the nineteenth century.

758. V. A. McClelland, *English Roman Catholics and higher education 1830–1903* (1973)

This account of the contribution of the Roman Catholic colleges to higher education is reduced in value by its author's partiality towards Manning (about whom he has previously written) and his resultant and deliberate underestimation of Newman's influence.

Technical Education

759. M. Argles, *South Kensington to Robbins. An account of English technical and scientific education since 1851* (1964)

760. G. W. Roderick and M. D. Stephens, *Scientific and technical education in nineteenth-century England: a symposium* (1973)

761. S. F. Cotgrove, *Technical education and social change* (1958)

There is no very readable study of this subject. **759** is a dull catalogue of information and **760** a collection of papers on certain limited aspects. The best brief introduction is contained in the early chapters of **761** though it is substantially concerned with the twentieth century.

Adult Education

762. T. Kelly, *A history of adult education in Great Britain* (1962; 2nd ed., 1970)

763. J. F. C. Harrison, *Learning and living 1790–1960: a study in the history of the English adult education movement* (1961)

764. M. Tylecote, *The Mechanics' Institutes of Lancashire and Yorkshire before 1851* (1957)

762, written by the biographer of George Birkbeck, a pioneer of

Education 125

adult education, is the fullest survey but it lacks the character and incisiveness of **763** confined though the latter is largely to adult education in Yorkshire in the last two centuries. **764** is an excellent study of the mechanics' institute movement and deserves a sequel on the post-1851 period.

7
RELIGION

The large number of books on nineteenth-century religious history is out of all proportion to the amount of time it currently occupies on undergraduate courses. The responsibility for this lies to a large extent with the Victorians who were zealous at making the Word, if not flesh, at least paper. And so the subject abounds with the sermons, precepts and pronouncements of divines eminent and obscure. Nor have latter-day Christians been remiss in contributing their own histories and biographies, and there is no shortage of monographs on religious bodies as different in their beliefs as Baptists and Moravians, the Salvation Army and the Jews. Even late-Victorian dabbling in psychical research has been examined. Most of this is, of course, only of interest to the specialist or the converted, and much of it is as dry as the paper on which it is written. The last decade or so has witnessed a movement away from institutional and towards religious social history, but it has not yet gone nearly far enough, and this branch of historical inquiry remains dogged by devotional and uncritical, not to say untheoretical, outpourings. Related topics considered elsewhere in this bibliography include the Victorian celebration of death [**529–30**], the tithe question [**409**], religious immigrant groups [**534–37**], secularism [**164–65**], and religion and urbanisation [several essays in **706**].

General

765. O. Chadwick, *The Victorian church* (2 vols., 1966–70; 2nd ed., 1972)

766. A. D. Gilbert, *Religion and society in industrial England: church, chapel and social change 1740–1914* (1976)

Scholars of church history relied for forty years on Elliott-Binns's introduction to religion in the Victorian era. It has now been replaced by Gilbert's excellent short survey. The *magnum opus* on nineteenth-century religion is, however, **765** which, despite its great length and its neglect of nonconformity, must be counted as essential reading for even the rawest of undergraduates. Its chapters on rural and urban religious life are particularly valuable.

Religion

767. A. Armstrong, *The Church of England, the Methodists, and society, 1700–1850* (1973)

768. W. R. Ward, *Religion and society in England, 1790–1850* (1972)

Two studies which, by emphasising dissent, counterbalance the Anglican bias of **765**—at least for the first half of the century. The novice will find **767** more easily digestible than **768** which assumes a certain amount of prior knowledge in the reader.

769. H. McLeod, *Class and religion in the late Victorian city* (1974)

An examination of the religious behaviour of three sections of London society in the period 1880–1914. This type of study, of the effects of religion on social change within particular communities, marks an important new departure in religious historiography. [Cf. **801**.]

770. A. O. J. Cockshut (ed.), *Religious controversies of the nineteenth century: selected documents* (1966)

771. L. W. Cowie, *Religion* (1973)

There is no single collection of documents which can be recommended for general use. **770** is a rather too particular selection, and **771** suffers from the general drawbacks of the 'Examining the evidence' series [see **307**].

772. B. M. G. Reardon, *From Coleridge to Gore. A century of religious thought in Britain* (1971)

773. B. Willey, *Nineteenth-century studies. Coleridge to Matthew Arnold* (1949; repr. 1964)

774. B. Willey, *More nineteenth-century studies: a group of honest doubters* (1956)

772 is a heavy-going catalogue of the major, and many of the minor, religious pundits. It is particularly unpalatable because it makes little attempt to relate developments in religious thought to the history of the period. But it is useful as a work of reference, for a summary of the ideas of particular divines. **773** and **774** are a series of interconnected essays concerned primarily, though not exclusively, with the religious and moral ideas and doubts of a number of prominent writers (e.g. Coleridge, Tennyson, George Eliot and Matthew Arnold), theologians (e.g. Newman, J. A. Froude, and other leaders of the Oxford Movement), teachers (e.g. Thomas Arnold), and politicians (e.g. John Morley).

775. A. Symondson (ed.), *The Victorian crisis of faith* (1970)

Six lectures of uneven quality. The most useful are those by R. M. Young on the impact of Darwin on conventional thought; Best on Evangelicalism; Newsome on Newman and the Oxford Movement; and Chadwick on the established church under attack. The remaining two are on Victorian missionaries, and the prayer book.

776. U. R. Q. Henriques, *Religious toleration in England, 1787–1833* (1961)

The best study of the struggles of dissenters, Catholics and minority groups for religious (and social and political) equality.

The Church of England

777. E. R. Norman, *Church and society in England 1770–1970: a historical study* (1976)

A review of Anglican social and political activity over the last two centuries in which the author's prejudices are scarcely disguised.

778. O. Brose, *Church and parliament: the reshaping of the Church of England, 1828–60* (1959)

779. D. Bowen, *The idea of the Victorian church: a study of the Church of England, 1833–89* (1968)

780. M. A. Crowther, *Church embattled: religious controversy in mid-Victorian England* (1969)

781. P. T. Marsh, *The Victorian church in decline. Archbishop Tait and the Church of England, 1868–82* (1969)

Four studies of the Church of England in an era of challenge and reform. **778** shows how it adapted in its relations with the state to survive the threat of disestablishment. **779** and **780** are unconvincing attempts at elucidating the role and vitality of the church in an era of rapid social change. The first seeks to demonstrate that it eased social tension by bridging the gap between aristocracy and bourgeoisie; the second that theological squabbles rendered it incapable of dealing with social reform. Both arguments seem to ignore fundamental aspects of the social and political structure. Although **781** focuses on the career of Tait, it is pertinent for its account of the clergy's unsure response to the collectivist drive and to the spiritual and dogmatic crisis created by the Darwinian revolution. [See also, **775**.]

782. D. L. Edwards, *Leaders of the Church of England, 1828–1944* (1971)

Based on printed sources, this is an eminently readable collection of portraits of twenty prominent Anglicans which provides not only an introduction to the history of the church, but also an admirable substitute for the weighty biographical tomes which it has used to good purpose.

783. A. Smith, *The established church and popular religion, 1750–1850* (1971)
One of the 'Seminar' pamphlets [see **70**].

784. D. Nicholls (ed.), *Church and state in Britain since 1820* (1967)
A collection of documents designed for undergraduates and concerned with contemporary critics and defenders of the principle of an established church.

Evangelicalism
[see also, **294–95** and **775**]

785. F. K. Brown, *Fathers of the Victorians. The age of Wilberforce* (1961)

786. K. Heasman, *Evangelicals in action: an appraisal of their social work in the Victorian era* (1962)

787. I. Bradley, *The call to seriousness. The evangelical impact on the Victorians* (1976)

785 and **786** are contrasting assessments of Evangelicalism. The first antipathetic and overlong, the second, symptomatic of its Ph.D. origins, a friendly account which claims too much for its subjects. **787** is a more balanced assessment, a hybrid of Brown's cynicism and Heasman's sympathy.

The Oxford Movement

788. D. Newsome, *The parting of friends: a study of the Wilberforces and Henry Manning* (1966)

789. O. Chadwick (ed.), *The mind of the Oxford Movement* (1960)

790. C. S. Dessain, *John Henry Newman* (1966)

There are many studies of the Oxford Movement and possibly still more biographies of Cardinal Newman, and yet none of them is entirely satisfactory. **789** is a collection of documents, but its introduction provides the best outline for students. **790** is a short biography written by the man who, until his death, was responsible for editing

Newman's letters and diaries. Undoubtedly the most stimulating study of early Victorian Anglicanism is **788** which succeeds in demonstrating why men went through the transition from Evangelicalism to the Oxford Movement and Roman Catholicism. [Cf. Newsome's essay in **775**.]

Roman Catholicism
[see also, **61** and **758**]

791. E. I. Watkin, *Roman Catholicism in England from the Reformation to 1950* (1957)

792. J. Bossy, *The English Catholic community 1570–1850* (1975)

793. G. A. Beck (ed.), *The English Catholics 1850–1950. Essays to commemorate the centenary of the restoration of the hierarchy of England and Wales* (1950)

791 is no more than a cursory outline. The third part of **792** provides a short introduction to Catholicism before the restoration of the hierarchy and must be supplemented by the essays in **793** for the later period. A satisfactory single volume of nineteenth-century Catholicism has yet to be written, though much can be gleaned from the biographies of Vaughan, Newman, Wiseman and Manning. The main deficiency is the absence of any general study of grass-roots Catholicism, although J. Hickey has made a useful start in a study centred on Cardiff.

794. E. R. Norman, *Anti-Catholicism in Victorian England* (1968)

Chooses four episodes (Maynooth, 1845; re-establishment of the hierarchy; opposition to Ritualism; and the trial of Bishop Edward King, 1890) to expound the theme of anti-Catholicism as a major religious and political catalyst. The book includes a selection of documents. A valuable beginning but it deals only patchily with anti-Catholic rioting (e.g. the Murphy riots) which requires further investigation. [Cf. the essay by Best in **53**.]

Nonconformity

795. D. M. Thompson (ed.), *Nonconformity in the nineteenth century* (1972)

796. J. H. Y. Briggs and I. Sellers (eds.), *Victorian nonconformity* (1973)

Religion

The most glaring gap in the study of nineteenth-century religion in Britain is the absence of an up-to-date account of nonconformity, and these two collections of quite different documents go only a little way towards filling it. Thompson's contribution to the 'Birth of modern Britain' series [see **576**] contains a good guide to further reading.

797. M. L. Edwards, *After Wesley: a study of the social and political influence of Methodism in the middle period [1791–1849]* (1935)

798. M. L. Edwards, *Methodism and England: a study of Methodism in its social and political aspects during the period 1850–1932* (1943)

799. J. Kent, *The age of disunity* (1966)

800. B. Semmel, *The Methodist revolution* (1974)

801. R. Moore, *Pit-men, preachers and politics: the effects of Methodism in a Durham mining community* (1974)

802. S. Koss, *Nonconformity in modern British politics* (1975)

Scholars of Methodism have greatly exaggerated its social and political importance. This is true of **797, 798** and **800**, as well as of the several studies by Wearmouth [see, for example, **807–9**] and the general interpretation of early nineteenth-century history by Halévy [see **3**]. Historians of the left have pushed the pendulum in the opposite direction [see **181** and **559**]. Recent narrow studies, such as that by T. Laqueur of the Sunday Schools which attacks **559**, indicate that the debate is far from dead. **799** does, however, attempt a more balanced assessment and is particularly useful for its account of the divisions within Victorian Methodism. **801** attempts to test the conclusions of both sides in the controversy through an examination of the social and political influence of Methodism in a small Durham community. And **802** establishes the reasons for the waning political power of the nonconformists, demonstrating the extent to which, for them, the Liberal victory of 1906 was a false dawn. [Cf. **168**.]

803. E. A. Isichei, *The Victorian Quakers* (1970)

A balanced account of this small but influential sect.

804. E. W. Gosse, *Father and son. A study of two temperaments* (1907; repr. 1964)

This fragment of autobiography offers excellent insight into the impact of Darwinian and scientific ideas on a fundamentalist

(Plymouth Brethren) household and the resultant tensions between father and son.

The Churches and Social Reform

805. R. G. Cowherd, *The politics of English Dissent. The religious aspects of liberal and humanitarian reform movements from 1815 to 1848* (1959)

806. R. Soloway, *Prelates and people: ecclesiastical social thought in England, 1783–1852* (1969)

The first provides a brief survey of the period between the end of the Napoleonic Wars and the demise of Chartism, the second a review of the response of the bishops to the social problems created by industrialisation. The organisational response of the established church to these problems has been examined by K. A. Thompson.

807. R. F. Wearmouth, *Methodism and the working-class movements of England, 1800–50* (1937)

808. R. F. Wearmouth, *Methodism and the struggle of the working classes, 1850–1900* (1954)

809. R. F. Wearmouth, *Some working-class movements of the nineteenth century* (1948)

His theme—the influence of Methodism on the conduct and organisation of the working-class movements—is overdone, in the sense that he ignores other and more important influences.

810. T. Christensen, *Origin and history of Christian Socialism, 1848–54* (1962)

811. P. d'A. Jones, *The Christian Socialist revival, 1877–1914. Religion, class and social conscience in late Victorian England* (1967)

810 is a sound critical assessment bringing out clearly the deficiencies of the movement during its most influential period in a way which **811** fails to do for its later history. There are also a handful of biographies of prominent Christian Socialists—notably J. M. Ludlow, Charles Kingsley, and F. D. Maurice.

812. K. S. Inglis, *Churches and the working classes in Victorian England* (1963)

813. S. Mayor, *The churches and the labour movement* (1967)

814. G. S. R. Kitson Clark, *Churchmen and the condition of England 1832–85* (1973)

The reaction of the churches to the 'condition of England' question, particularly in the post-Chartist period, has only recently begun to be examined. **812** considers the churches' unsuccessful response to poor working-class attendance, and **813** their uneasy relationship with the embryonic labour movement. But **814** points to the many questions still left unanswered.

8
WALES, SCOTLAND AND IRELAND

For too long now, the British history courses taught in England have been essentially English history courses. Welsh history has been bracketed with English, Ireland has been studied only in so far as it was a nuisance to its English rulers, while Scottish differences are usually ignored. The responsibility for this must be borne not only by English teachers but by Celtic historians as well. They have written too exclusively in terms of the political relationship with England, and only in recent years has there been any serious move towards social, cultural and intellectual inquiry. Wales has been the most neglected. There are a number of articles and books in the Welsh language but it would be a great proselytising mission on the part of nationalist historians were they to produce social and cultural history accessible to an English readership and pointing the uniqueness of the Welsh past. Scotland has fared slightly better. The educational and religious aspects of its social history have been well charted, and certain parts of its economic history more than adequately studied. (There is, for example, a long and heavygoing but probably definitive study by Checkland of Scottish banking.) However, much remains to be done in terms of working-class movements. Ireland has received the fullest treatment of all, and there are few gaps in its political, and less of late in its economic, history. There are, for example, detailed monographs on the Catholic emancipation crisis in Ireland in the 1820s, the Independent Irish party in the 1850s, Orangeism and Fenianism, the Ulster crisis of 1910–18, the land question and the Land League crisis, police reform in the wake of rural disorder, 1812–36, the banking system in the early part of the century, emigration, and even a study of the Guinness brewery. The most prominent Irish leaders have received a modern treatment—Redmond, Carson, Dillon, Casement, Collins, and Connolly—but not yet Michael Davitt or Tim Healy. And Young Ireland deserves a more up-to-date treatment than that afforded by Dennis Gwynn. The main weakness is, however, the failure to come to grips with the rural base, that is the peasantry; we have several histories of Irish nationalism rather than the Irish people. But as the gaps are steadily filled the failure to make British history courses what they claim to be becomes less and less pardonable.

General

815. M. Hechter, *Internal colonialism. The Celtic fringe in British national development, 1536–1966* (1975)

Uses the Celtic fringe as a model for his 'internal colony' thesis to explain why national differences have triumphed over the centripetal forces associated with the modern industrial world.

Wales

(a) GENERAL

816. D. Williams, *A history of modern Wales* (1950)

817. A. J. Roderick (ed.), *Wales through the ages. Vol. ii: Modern Wales* (1960; repr. 1973)

816 has been the standard general survey for a generation, a reflection not so much of its intrinsic merit, though it is good, but of the dearth of competition. 817 is a collection of twenty-seven radio talks dealing briefly with the major aspects of Welsh history. For background information, the *Dictionary of Welsh biography* (1959) merits occasional consultation.

(b) POLITICAL

818. T. Evans, *The background of modern Welsh politics 1789–1846* (1936)

819. K. O. Morgan, *Wales in British politics, 1868–1922* (1963; 2nd ed., 1970)

Evans's study of the growth of political consciousness in Wales in the first half of the nineteenth century has now been superseded in large parts by 827, 828 and 836. Morgan's is a much needed look at Welsh issues in the British parliament and the mainly nonconformist activists (not least of all, Lloyd George) who promoted them. It is excellent on Welsh politics, but tells us little of the social background to this efflorescence of Welsh Liberalism.

(c) ECONOMIC

820. B. Thomas (ed.), *The Welsh economy. Studies in expansion* (1962)

821. A. H. Dodd, *The industrial revolution in North Wales* (1933; 3rd ed., 1971)

822. A. H. John, *The industrial development of South Wales 1750–1850. An essay* (1950)

823. W. E. Minchinton (ed.), *Industrial South Wales 1750–1914. Essays in Welsh economic history* (1969)

Writing on the Welsh economy has been patchy and spasmodic and there is no single coherent survey of its modern history, but **821** and **822** together cover the early part of the period reasonably well. The essays in **820** focus on the twentieth century, though they do in part refer back to the second half of the nineteenth. The journal articles in **823** are rather specialised, but Minchinton's introduction merits early perusal by students as a short guide to the industrial history of South Wales before the first world war.

824. J. H. Morris and L. J. Williams, *The South Wales coal industry, 1841–75* (1958)

825. E. W. Evans, *The miners of South Wales* (1961)

826. E. W. Evans, *Mabon: a study of trade union leadership* (1959)

The emphasis of **824** on the economic organisation of the industry and of **825** on trade unionism are both welcome as far as they go, but neither brings a social dimension to their examination of the close-knit mining communities of South Wales. As the sub-title of **826** suggests, it is not a biography but a study of William Abraham's leadership of the South Wales miners, and again is satisfactory as far as its limited objective permits.

(d) SOCIAL [for religion, see **924**]

827. D. J. V. Jones, *Before Rebecca. Popular protests in Wales 1793–1835* (1973)

828. D. Williams, *The Rebecca riots: a study in agrarian unrest* (1955)

The first, a series of case-studies of popular disturbances in the late eighteenth and early nineteenth centuries and with a short concluding chapter in which Jones analyses the causes, character and significance of the riots, and the second, a full account of the agrarian demonstrations in West Wales in the 1830s and 1840s, are distinguished contributions not only to Welsh social history but also to our understanding of 'primitive' protest movements. [See also, **551**.] It is instructive to compare these two books with David Jenkins's study of the agricultural community in south-west Wales at the turn of the present century when rural society was undergoing the changes wrought by mechanisation.

829. D. C. A. Bradshaw (ed.), *Studies in the government and control of education since 1860* (1970)

Although not specifically confined to Wales, this collection of papers on educational administration includes one by L. W. Evans on Welsh education 1881–1921 which is particularly valuable in view of the paucity of studies of the subject.

Scotland

(a) GENERAL

830. J. D. Mackie, *A history of Scotland* (1964)

There are a fair number of popular general histories of Scotland. This has the advantage of being a readily available and cheap paperback. Its text is short but on the whole well-balanced.

831. G. S. Pryde, *Scotland from 1603 to the present day* (1962)

832. W. Ferguson, *Scotland, 1689 to the present day* (1968)

833. T. C. Smout, *A history of the Scottish people, 1560–1830* (1969)

There is no general history of Scotland in the nineteenth century to match Smout's account of the period down to 1830. Ferguson's is the best available, but like Pryde's, leaves important areas, particularly in the realm of economic and social history, unexplored.

834. C. W. Hill, *Edwardian Scotland* (1976)

A popular history aimed, perhaps, at cashing in on the current vogue for 'Edwardianism'.

835. G. Donaldson (ed.), *Scottish historical documents* (1970)

A chronological arrangement which provides back-up material to the general histories.

(b) POLITICAL

836. R. Coupland, *Welsh and Scottish nationalism: a study* (1954)

837. H. J. Hanham, *Scottish nationalism* (1969)

Both books place present-day nationalism soundly in its historical context. [See also, Hanham's shorter introduction to the subject in **53**.]

(c) ECONOMIC

838. W. H. Marwick, *Scotland in modern times. An outline of economic and social development since the Union of 1707* (1964)

839. R. H. Campbell, *Scotland since 1707. The rise of an industrial society* (1965)

840. S. G. E. Lythe and J. Butt, *An economic history of Scotland 1100–1939* (1975)

841. R. H. Campbell and J. B. A. Dow (eds.), *Source book of Scottish economic and social history* (1968)

Marwick, who thirty years earlier had written an account of the economy in Victorian Scotland, here provides a shorter and more up-to-date introduction for the newcomer to Scottish economic and social history. The second part of **840** is an unobjectionable alternative. But undoubtedly the best general economic and social history of Scotland since the Union is Campbell's wide-ranging survey. **841** is a selection of documents illustrating much the same theme and period, but exemplifying in the very brief comments of the compilers an all-too-familiar shortcoming.

842. H. Hamilton, *The industrial revolution in Scotland* (1932; repr. 1966)

Concentrates on the two major stages in Scotland's economic development from the preponderance of cotton to its supersession by the metal industries after 1830, but embraces also the agricultural revolution. Given its particular emphases, it is well worth its reprint.

843. A. Slaven, *The development of the west of Scotland, 1750–1960* (1975)

The first in a projected new series of regional economic and social histories aimed at undergraduates and summarising recent research, this is a good start though it is stronger on the economic than the social.

844. T. B. Franklin, *A history of Scottish farming* (1952)

845. J. A. Symon, *Scottish farming, past and present* (1959)

The first provides a cursory, the second a comprehensive, treatment of modern Scottish farming.

846. J. Hunter, *The making of the crofting community* (1976)

Extensively researched and based on a doctoral thesis on the Highland crofting community, it supersedes the few chapters of historical background in A. Collier's earlier treatment of the crofting problem. [For Highland discontent, see **551** and **588**.]

847. M. Gray, *The Highland economy 1750–1850* (1956)

848. P. Gaskell, *Morvern transformed: a Highland parish in the nineteenth century* (1968)

Like Williams's study of the Rebecca riots [**828**] and accounts of the Irish economy and of the famine [for example, **903**], **847** delineates clearly the stresses created within a feudal economy by proximity to a powerful industrial neighbour. **848**'s study of a remote parish on the west coast of Scotland is far from being the narrow affair its title might suggest. Instead, it throws light on the social and economic transformations effected by changes in land-ownership in the nineteenth century.

(d) SOCIAL

849. T. Ferguson, *The dawn of Scottish social welfare* (1948)

850. T. Ferguson, *Scottish social welfare, 1864–1914* (1958)

851. L. J. Saunders, *Scottish democracy 1815–40. The social and intellectual background* (1950)

The two volumes by Ferguson (the second covering only fifty years is double the length of the first), are the standard account of social welfare and show clearly the differences between Scottish and English conditions. He does, however, neglect the social and intellectual climate which prepared the way for reform and which is lucidly described by Saunders, at least for the period 1815–40 and particularly for education.

852. H. M. Knox, *Two hundred and fifty years of Scottish education, 1696–1946* (1953)

853. J. Scotland, *The history of Scottish education* (2 vols., 1970)

854. G. E. Davie, *The democratic intellect: Scotland and her universities in the nineteenth century* (1961)

Studies of Scottish elementary education show the same deficiencies as those of English, except that while the latter are being remedied those of the former remain largely untouched. **852** is a prize example of 'blue book' history, concerned with legislation and change from above but eschewing the social dimension. **853**'s two-volume survey, divided at 1872, is the fullest history but at its most unsatisfactory on the nineteenth century. However, the story of the

Scottish universities' struggle to preserve their broadly democratic entry at the time when English universities were unashamedly elitist is extraordinarily well-told by Davie. [See also, **713**.]

855. T. Johnston, *The history of the working classes in Scotland* (1920; 4th ed., 1946; repr. 1974)

856. W. H. Marwick, *A short history of labour in Scotland* (1967)

The working-class movement in Scotland has been sadly neglected. One or two narrow studies, for example of trade unionism in Aberdeen and of the insurrection in the Scottish lowlands in 1820, are now beginning to appear, but the only extant general histories are the thin account by Marwick and the dated and polemical collection of essays by Johnston.

857. L. C. Wright, *Scottish Chartism* (1953)

858. A. Wilson, *The Chartist movement in Scotland* (1970)

Although the conclusions of **857** are broadly sound and unobjectionable, it ranks more as an interim report when compared with the exhaustive and meticulous research of **858**.

(e) RELIGION

859. J. H. S. Burleigh, *A church history of Scotland* (1960)

860. A. L. Drummond and J. Bulloch, *The Scottish church 1688–1843: the age of the moderates* (1973)

861. A. L. Drummond and J. Bulloch, *The church in Victorian Scotland, 1843–74* (1975)

862. S. Mechie, *The church and Scottish social development, 1780–1870* (1960)

Not surprisingly, the Scottish (like the English) church has attracted a disproportionate share of historical attention. The narrative of **860** and **861**, constructed by Bulloch from manuscripts left by the late A. L. Drummond, provides the fullest survey [a sort of Scottish Chadwick—see **765**]. **859**, however, is a shorter and adequate alternative, and where it is weak on certain denominations such as the Episcopalians and the Roman Catholics there are monographs on these subjects to lighten our darkness. **862** only begins to explore the social work of Scottish Christians in the nineteenth century, but it is Mechie's stated intention to upturn just a few stones in order to tempt other historians to examine the rest.

Ireland
[see also, **61, 87** and **537–39**]

(a) GENERAL

863. J. C. Beckett, *A short history of Ireland* (1952; 5th ed., 1973)

864. O. MacDonagh, *Ireland* (1968)

865. R. D. Edwards, *A new history of Ireland* (1972)

Beckett's survey is still unsurpassed as a short introduction despite its old-fashioned political emphasis, though Edwards's two chapters on the nineteenth century in **865** are a satisfactory substitute. The most stimulating introduction is, however, MacDonagh's interpretative essay on modern Irish history.

866. J. C. Beckett, *The making of modern Ireland, 1603–1923* (1966)

867. F. S. L. Lyons, *Ireland since the famine* (1971)

868. E. R. Norman, *A history of modern Ireland* (1971)

Beckett's more concentrated study of the modern period is, like his general survey, excellent on political but weak on economic and social history. The main strength of **867** also is its political narrative though Lyons does give the nod to recent developments in Irish historiography by including sections on economic, social and cultural history, and, together with its very good bibliography these factors make it the best general history of modern Ireland. The air of old-fashioned English superiority towards the Irish which pervades **868** has more in common with nineteenth-century historiography than with modern scholarship, and aroused the ire of nationalist historians when it was first published.

869. K. Marx and F. Engels, *On Ireland* (1971)

A compilation comprised mainly of their letters on the Irish question from the 1840s to (in Engels's case) the 1890s.

870. T. W. Moody and J. C. Beckett (eds.), *Ulster since 1800. Vol. i: a political and economic survey*; *Vol. ii: a social survey* (1954–57)

871. T. W. Moody, *The Ulster question, 1603–1973* (1974)

The two volumes of **870** are composed of thirty-four very short radio-talks by prominent Irish scholars on many aspects of Ulster's modern history. And **871**, though primarily an analysis of the contemporary situation in Ulster, does also provide one of the most concise and illuminating accounts of its historical roots.

872. E. Curtis and R. B. McDowell (eds.), *Irish historical documents 1172–1922* (1943)

873. J. Carty (comp. and ed.), *Ireland from Grattan's parliament to the great famine (1783–1850): a documentary record* (1952)

874. J. Carty (comp. and ed.), *Ireland from the great famine to the treaty (1851–1921): a documentary record* (1951)

Irish historians have been strangely reluctant to jump on the anthology-bandwagon and so we have still to make do with these old compilations. The first in particular reflects the period of its composition in its leaning to political documentation, and in many respects the two volumes by Carty are more useful and less insipid in that they include accounts of social as well as political events and are illustrated.

(b) POLITICAL [see also, **167**]

875. L. J. McCaffrey *The Irish question, 1800–1922* (1968)

876. P. O'Farrell, *England and Ireland since 1800* (1975)

877. P. O'Farrell, *Ireland's English question: Anglo-Irish relations 1534–1970* (1971)

878. E. Strauss, *Irish nationalism and British democracy* (1951)

879. K. B. Nowlan, *The politics of repeal: a study in the relations between Great Britain and Ireland, 1841–50* (1965)

880. P. N. S. Mansergh, *The Irish question 1840–1921: a commentary on Anglo-Irish relations and on social and political forces in Ireland in the age of reform and revolution* (1965; 3rd ed., 1975)

881. G. Dangerfield, *The damnable question. A study in Anglo-Irish relations* (1976)

The political implications of the Union have for too long been almost the sole preoccupation of Irish historians. **875** is a good and recent example of this type of political narrative. O'Farrell who, in **877**, saw Catholicism as fundamental to the nature of the relationship, has since developed his thesis into a thought-provoking analysis of the irreconcilable stereotypes and prejudices underlying that relationship (**876**). **878** was an early and isolated attempt to dig beneath the political and social manifestations of the Union to its solid economic base. **879** is a scholarly analysis of the relationship in the era of Daniel O'Connell, and **880** an enlarged and revised version, taking account of recent scholarship, of the author's stimulating essay *Ireland in the age of reform and revolution* (1940). **881** centres on the Easter rising of 1916 and the extent to which it marked a watershed in Anglo-Irish relations.

882. R. B. McDowell, *The Irish administration, 1801–1914* (1964)

A well-written piece of administrative history surveying the government departments established to administer the Union.

883. R. Kee, *The green flag: a history of Irish nationalism* (1972)

A long (over 750 pages) and labyrinthine account of its subject, fascinating to read but offering little analysis of the phenomenon he describes so well.

884. R. B. McDowell, *Public opinion and government policy in Ireland, 1801–46* (1952)

885. A. Macintyre, *The liberator: Daniel O'Connell and the Irish party, 1830–47* (1965)

886. R. D. Edwards, *Daniel O'Connell and his world* (1975)

O'Connell looms large in **884** even though its subject matter is more general, and his politics are admirably analysed in **885** which, together with **879**, provides a full history of the Repeal Party. **886** is a very short, popular, and lavishly illustrated account of O'Connell and his times. [See also, Treble's essay in **587**.]

887. E. D. Steele, *Irish land and British politics* (1974)

888. L. J. McCaffrey, *Irish federalism in the 1870s. A study in conservative nationalism* (1962)

889. D. Thornley, *Isaac Butt and home rule* (1964)

The story of the federal movement led by Isaac Butt is told with compactness and style by McCaffrey, qualities sadly absent from Thornley's unnecessarily long narrative. Gladstone's Irish Land Act is subjected to microscopic analysis by Steele in a rather old-fashioned study which is stronger on British politics than the Irish context.

890. T. Corfe, *The Phoenix Park murders: conflict, compromise and tragedy in Ireland, 1879–82* (1968)

891. J. L. Hammond, *Gladstone and the Irish nation* (1938; repr. 1964)

Corfe's is not, as his title might suggest, simply a sensational account of the murders but a reasoned survey of the background against which they took place. Hammond's study is crucial to an understanding both of Gladstone's policy and of the Irish question in the period 1868–94, and was deservedly reprinted in 1964.

892. F. S. L. Lyons, *Charles Stewart Parnell* (1977)

893. F. S. L. Lyons, *Parnell* (1963; repr. 1965)

894. C. C. O'Brien, *Parnell and his party 1880–90* (1957)

895. M. Hurst, *Parnell and Irish nationalism* (1968)

896. F. S. L. Lyons, *The fall of Parnell, 1890–91* (1960)

Lyons has undoubtedly made himself the foremost authority on Parnell. Having already written a detailed account of the O'Shea divorce case and Parnell's downfall (**896**) and an excellent short introduction to the Irish leader's life in a Dublin Historical Association pamphlet (**893**), he has now produced an outstanding and probably definitive biography (**892**)—which partly renders O'Brien's otherwise excellent account of Parnellite politics redundant (**894**) and certainly does so to Hurst's shadowy outline (**895**). It also overshadowed an interesting study of Parnell's family background by R. Foster which appeared at much the same time.

897. F. S. L. Lyons, *The Irish parliamentary party, 1890–1910* (1951)
A detailed analysis based on extensive research.

898. L. P. Curtis Jr., *Coercion and conciliation in Ireland, 1880–92: a study in Conservative Unionism* (1963)

899. P. Buckland, *Irish Unionism. Vol. i: The Anglo-Irish and the new Ireland, 1885–1922*; *Vol. ii: Ulster Unionism and the origins of Northern Ireland, 1886–1922* (1972–73)

900. P. Buckland, *Irish Unionism, 1885–1923: a documentary history* (1973)

901. P. Buckland, *Irish Unionism, 1885–1922* (1973)

902. P. Gibbon, *The origins of Ulster Unionism. The formation of popular Protestant politics and ideology in nineteenth-century Ireland* (1975)

Although Buckland has made the study of Irish Unionism very much his own—his two-volume history and the volume of supportive documents form a very comprehensive history, and his Historical Association pamphlet on the subject (**901**) is a useful summary of his researches—there is still much of value to be found in **898**, particularly concerning Balfour's tenure of the Irish secretaryship, while Gibbon demonstrates that the subject can still be approached in a new and refreshing manner, though his Marxist interpretation will no doubt irritate many of his readers.

(c) ECONOMIC

903. R. D. C. Black, *Economic thought and the Irish question, 1817–70* (1960)

904. L. M. Cullen, *An economic history of Ireland since 1660* (1972)

The neglect of non-political aspects of Irish history is reflected in the fact that we have had to wait until 1972 for a survey of economic development, and **904** is therefore a welcome synthesis of recent research as well as an indicator of terrain still to be traversed. **903** is an important study of a narrower period which by disclosing the inadequacy of applying English economic theory to Irish conditions brings out clearly the disadvantages for an underdeveloped economy of union with a highly developed one. Black has also done future economic historians a great service by including in his book a lengthy bibliography.

905. R. D. Crotty, *Irish agricultural production. Its volume and structure* (1966)

Although two-thirds of the book is concerned with the period after 1922, the chapters on the nineteenth century offer a major revaluation of Irish agricultural history, particularly of orthodox interpretations of the famine as a significant watershed. But his claim that it caused 'hardly a tremor' in agricultural and demographic trends stretches both the evidence and our credulity.

906. B. L. Solow, *The land question and the Irish economy, 1870–1903* (1971)

907. J. S. Donnelly Jr., *The land and people of nineteenth-century Cork. The rural economy and the land question* (1975)

Both these books take up some of the issues raised by Crotty concerning the system of land tenure and its contribution to Ireland's economic problems in the post-famine period, the latter through a detailed study of County Cork.

908. A. Boyd, *The rise of the Irish trade unions 1729–1970* (1972)

An outline at times oversimplified and far from being the rigorous study which the subject requires.

909. B. Inglis, *The freedom of the press in Ireland 1784–1841* (1954)

A little less than half is concerned with the period after 1815. It describes the conflict between the Irish press and the English government and the evolution in relations between them from repression to the relative tranquillity during Melbourne's administration. This study remains important because the subject has been otherwise neglected.

(d) SOCIAL

910. G. O. Tuathaigh, *Ireland before the famine, 1798–1848* (1972)

911. J. Lee, *The modernization of Irish society, 1848–1918* (1973)

912. R. B. McDowell (ed.), *Social life in Ireland 1800–45* (1957)

Just as **904** filled a gap in Irish economic history, the two competent general textbooks by Tuathaigh and Lee (both volumes in the 'Gill History of Ireland') have begun the task of doing the same for social history, and in an equally enterprising and welcome manner. The collection of short essays in **912** were no more than an interim stop-gap, covering such topics as the country house, travel, the army, rural life, education, and Dublin and Belfast, and including short summaries by their authors of themes they have treated more fully elsewhere—for example, Connell on population (cf. **913**) and Inglis on the press (cf. **909**).

913. K. H. Connell, *The population of Ireland 1750–1845* (1950)

Demonstrates the crucial role of the potato in both the rapid increase in population and its decimation by the famine. His thesis has not, however, gone unchallenged in the journals, and the subsequent debate has demonstrated the need for more research to follow up the conclusions of Connell, and also of R. N. Salaman who has written in more general terms about the social influence of the potato.

914. R. D. Edwards and T. D. Williams (eds.), *The great famine* (1957)

915. C. Woodham-Smith, *The great hunger. Ireland 1845–9* (1962)

There is still no entirely satisfactory appraisal of the consequences of this cataclysmic event in Irish history. Some of the scholars who contributed essays to **914** have merely summarised some of the views which they have developed at greater length elsewhere, but it is a valuable symposium for all that. Woodham-Smith did not seize the opportunity to explore some of the lines of inquiry suggested in **913**, but she does to perfection what she is extremely good at—that is, telling the story.

916. W. A. Maguire, *The Downshire estates in Ireland 1801–45. The management of Irish landed estates in the early nineteenth century* (1972)

Although Maguire is primarily concerned with only one large estate and within a quite short period of time his book nevertheless provides the basis for a reappraisal of Irish landlordism, and his conclusions, however tentative, are suggestive and important.

917. J. J. Auchmuty, *Irish education. A historical survey* (1937)

918. D. H. Akenson, *The Irish education experiment: the national system of education in the nineteenth century* (1969)

919. N. Atkinson, *Irish education: a history of educational institutions* (1969)

917 is dated but contains a useful chapter on Sir Thomas Wyse, and **919** is typical of much writing on education in its confinement to details of administrative and institutional progress. Undoubtedly the finest venture into the field of Irish educational history in the nineteenth century is **918**'s analysis of the national elementary system, which blends the usual administrative history with the social and political background.

920. K. H. Connell, *Irish peasant society: four historical essays* (1968)

The apparently abstruse nature of the topics considered by Connell in his four essays—illicit distillation, ether-drinking in Ulster, illegitimacy before the famine, and Catholicism and marriage in the century after the famine—partly disguises the fact that his book stands alone as the one serious attempt so far to examine the way of life of the Irish peasantry.

921. P. B. Ellis, *The history of the Irish working class* (1972)

922. A. Mitchell, *Labour in Irish politics, 1890–1930: the Irish labour movement in an age of revolution* (1974)

923. J. W. Boyle (ed.), *Leaders and workers* (1966)

The study of Irish labour has lagged behind that of the English movement, and **921**'s general survey of four hundred years, intended as a sequel to the old account by James Connolly, is at times too polemical to be entirely satisfactory. However, **922** is a serious examination of a short but important period—the period which saw the formation of the Irish Labour party. **923** contains lectures on eight Irish labour leaders including James Larkin, whose story has also been told in a full-length biography (by E. Larkin).

(e) RELIGION

924. P. M. H. Bell, *Disestablishment in Ireland and Wales* (1969)

925. R. B. McDowell, *The Church of Ireland 1869–1969* (1975)

Curiously enough there is no satisfactory single-volume survey of nineteenth-century Irish religion. **924** is an enterprising and scholarly account of the disestablishment debates in both Ireland and Wales, and **925** is more than equal to the task of conducting the story of the disestablished church through its first centenary.

926. E. R. Norman, *The Catholic Church and Ireland in the age of rebellion, 1859–73* (1965)

927. E. R. Norman, *The Catholic Church and Irish politics in the eighteen-sixties* (1965)

928. D. W. Miller, *Church, state and nation in Ireland, 1898–1921* (1973)

926 and **928** are detailed studies of the Catholic Church and politics, the conclusions of the first fortunately summarised for the student in a Dublin Historical Association pamphlet (**927**).

9
LITERARY AND CULTURAL

This concluding section is intended only as a very brief guide to some of the most central reading in literary and cultural studies which the student of nineteenth-century history will find rewarding. The literature of the period merits a critical bibliography of its own (the *Oxford history of English literature* is a voluminous study currently in progress), but those who require a short guide are advised to consult the article by A. S. Crehan, 'Victorian literature: materials for teaching and study (Great Britain)' in *Victorian Studies*, XIX (March, 1976). Nor is it my intention to review here books on art, architecture, music, the fine arts, science, philosophy, or even on nineteenth-century historians such as Macaulay and Acton, or prominent critics such as Ruskin. Many of the books included in Section 5 provide some introduction to these topics. [See, for example, **497–501, 513** and **706**.]

929. B. Ford (ed.), *The Pelican guide to English literature. Vol. v: From Blake to Byron*; *Vol. vi: From Dickens to Hardy* (1957–58)
Useful starting-points which provide bibliographical and biographical information as well as short surveys of the best-known literature.

930. W. Walsh, *The use of imagination: educational thought and the literary mind* (1959; repr. 1966)
A brilliant study of the educational ideas of a number of prominent writers including Coleridge, Wordsworth, Keats, Hopkins, Yeats and Lawrence.

931. H. Jackson, *The eighteen-nineties: a review of art and ideas at the close of the nineteenth century* (1913; repr. 1976)
A stimulating analysis of the art and literature of the 1890s which has been justly reprinted numerous times, and most recently in 1976.

932. A. C. Kettle, *An introduction to the English novel* (2 vols., 1951–53)

933. F. R. Leavis, *The great tradition: George Eliot, Henry James, Joseph Conrad* (1948; repr. 1962)

934. K. Tillotson, *Novels of the eighteen-forties* (1954)

935. L. Cazamian, *The social novel in England 1830–50: Dickens, Disraeli, Mrs Gaskell, Kingsley* (1903; trans. 1973)

936. H. House, *The Dickens world* (1941; 2nd ed., 1942; repr. 1960)

937. A. Fleishman, *The English historical novel: Walter Scott to Virginia Woolf* (1971)

938. P. J. Keating, *The working classes in Victorian fiction* (1971)

The title of **932** states its purpose admirably and is the best all-round introduction to the major novels, particularly those of that 'great tradition' identified and justified by Leavis. By contrast, **934** and **935** are concerned with the 'condition of England' novels, Cazamian's classic study being at last available in English after seventy years. The emphasis of **936** is as much on the society in which Dickens lived and upon which he drew for inspiration as it is on the novelist himself, his views on reform and the value of his novels as records of nineteenth-century social history. **937** is a theoretical discourse on the historical element in important works of English fiction, and **938** considers the changing attitude of novelists to the working classes from their preoccupation with the evils of industrialisation in the 1840s to the refinement of 'urban' fiction in the late nineteenth century.

939. M. Arnold, *Culture and anarchy* (1869; ed. J. Dover Wilson, 1932; repr. 1960)

940. R. Williams, *Culture and society, 1780–1950* (1958)

941. J. H. Buckley, *The Victorian temper. A study in literary culture* (1952)

942. C. Harvie, G. Martin and A. Scharf (eds.), *Industrialisation and culture, 1830–1914* (1970)

A list of essential reading on the culture of nineteenth-century Britain would be incomplete without Matthew Arnold's stringent critique of the endemic philistinism of a rapidly expanding industrial society. **940** is a path-finding study of social criticism and the development of the idea of culture since the 1780s, and **941** a thought-provoking search for the underlying forces of nineteenth-century culture and an excellent introduction to many minor, as well as some of the usual major, writers. **942**, an anthology which includes drawings, paintings and photographs, embodies the various talents of teachers of different disciplines—history, literature, and the fine arts—and was specifically designed for the Open University's foundation course in Humanities.

943. M. Vicinus, *The industrial muse. A study of nineteenth-century British working-class literature* (1974)

944. R. Colls, *The collier's rant. Song and culture in the industrial village* (1977)

Literature produced by rather than for the working classes is at last being seriously studied, and Vicinus makes sensible use of their broadsheets, poetry, music-hall routines, and so on to present a rewarding analysis of a unique phase of genuinely working-class culture before the advent of commercialism. The central theme of **944** is the interaction of community and culture in the mining villages of the north-east, and more local studies of this sort are imperative before some of the broader generalisations attempted by Vicinus can be properly tested.

945. R. K. Webb, *The British working-class reader, 1790–1848. Literacy and social tension* (1955)

946. R. D. Altick, *The English common reader: a social history of the mass reading public* (1957)

947. L. James, *Fiction for the working man, 1830–50: a study of the literature produced for the working classes in early Victorian urban England* (1963; repr. 1974)

948. L. James (ed.), *Print and the people 1819–51* (1976)

A number of books which paved the way for a study of popular culture by examining the literature produced for a mass readership in the wake of technological and educational progress. Webb is primarily concerned with the literature written in response to social problems, Altick with the readership itself, and James with a wide range of material produced for popular consumption, some of which he has gathered together in an exceptionally well-illustrated anthology (**948**).

APPENDIX A: ADDENDA

(The numbering of the sections is the same as that employed in the main body of the book.)

2. Political and Constitutional

GENERAL

A1. D. A. Hamer, *The politics of electoral pressure. A study in the history of Victorian reform agitations* (1977)

The first detailed examination of the ways in which pressure-groups—and, in particular, four major ones (the Anti-Corn Law League, the Liberation Society, the National Education League, and the United Kingdom Alliance)—applied pressure at parliamentary elections to persuade the political parties (but especially the Liberal party) to favour their causes. The book is intended to complement, by focusing on the grass-roots (or 'faddists'), the high politics of **153**, but is also an important corollary to Vincent **[152]** and to the accounts of the individual pressure-groups [see **54–56**].

A2. T. L. Crosby, *English farmers and the politics of protection 1815–52* (1977)

It has been assumed for too long that English farmers, because of their dependence upon good relations with their landlords, were inevitably a deferential electorate, and this book is the first serious attempt to test that assumption. It is reproduced direct from camera-ready typescript—an enterprising attempt to make scholarly works available at a viable price. It must be said, however, that while this method may help one's pocket, the size of type used here is not calculated to do the same for one's eyesight!

POLITICAL PARTIES

(e) *Labour*

A3. L. Middleton (ed.), *Women in the labour movement. The British experience* (1977)

A collection of essays divided into two parts, the first historical and the second concerned with the contemporary labour movement. The historical essays are tentative and offer little more than an introduction to a subject which is attracting increasing attention and where there is much work currently in the pipeline.

3. Foreign, Imperial and Defence

FOREIGN POLICY

(b) *Monographs*

A4. Z. S. Steiner, *Britain and the origins of the first world war* (1977)

Steiner has followed up her study of the foreign office in the pre-war period [see **318**] with this up-to-date account of British foreign policy from Queen Victoria's death to the outbreak of war in 1914. In asking whether the principal determinant of that policy was domestic strife or external considerations, she unreservedly plumps for the latter. But, despite her painstaking use of a wide range of both primary and secondary materials, her conclusions are neither very startling nor very new.

IMPERIALISM

(c) *Monographs*

A5. D. C. M. Platt (ed.), *Business imperialism 1840–1930. An inquiry based on British experience in Latin America* (1977)

A collection of narrow empirical studies of British business interests in Latin America concerning finance, public utilities and transport, and trade, as well as case-studies of the relations between certain British companies and Latin American governments.

4. Economic

TRADE UNIONS AND LABOUR RELATIONS

A6. S. Lewenhak, *Women and trade unions. An outline history of women in the British trade union movement* (1977)

The 'outline' of the title is the operative word. The contents provide a rather dull catalogue of information concentrating, like much of the recent work on women in the labour movement [cf. **A3**], on the activities of a number of individuals.

5. Social

URBAN SOCIETY

(c) *Class relationships*

A7. A. P. Donajgrodzki (ed.), *Social control in nineteenth-century Britain* (1977)

An important new book—a collection of nine essays which seek to apply the concept of social control drawn from sociology to the relationship between rich and poor in nineteenth-century Britain. Amongst the mechanisms of social control discussed are the police, education, religion, leisure, and charity. The editor's introduction is an excellent vindication of this methodology.

SOCIAL REFORM

(d) *Public health*

A8. F. F. Cartwright, *A social history of medicine* (1977)

A9. J. Woodward and D. Richards (eds.), *Health care and popular medicine in nineteenth-century England. Essays in the social history of medicine* (1977)

The recent appearance of these two books marks a major advance in our knowledge of the sociology of nineteenth-century medicine. Cartwright's is an important but incomplete treatise—it does not move far enough in the directions of its title and away from being a conventional history of social medicine, but far enough to make it the best available introduction to the subject. The terrain which remains to be explored is indicated in the introduction to the collection of essays in **A8** which concentrates on two particular themes—knowledge of sex and sexuality, and professionalisation in medicine. Indeed, the first essay reviews the current state of our knowledge of the social aspects of medical history, and is a good introduction to the available literature on the subject.

(f) *Crime and punishment*

A10. W. R. Miller, *Cops and bobbies. Police authority in New York and London, 1830–70* (1977)

Important for the type of questions which are posed (particularly concerning the extent to which the police force was a middle-class institution) rather than for its examination of the roots of the different types of police authority in London and New York. It includes a very useful and up-to-date bibliography and supplements Critchley [689] which has little on the metropolitan police.

6. Education

ELEMENTARY AND SECONDARY

A11. P. McCann (ed.), *Popular education and socialization in the nineteenth-century* (1977)

A collection of nine essays which 'explores ways in which various types of elementary education, at different periods of the nineteenth century, attempted to prepare the working-class child for life and labour in industrial capitalist society'. A further and refreshing indication of the move by historians of education away from institutional and administrative history. The contributors employ the sociological concept of socialisation to investigate education at the grass-roots level, and their conclusions should be compared with the observations on social control in **A7**.

7. Religion

NONCONFORMITY

A12. C. Binfield, *So down to prayers. Studies in English nonconformity 1780–1920* (1977)

Not the much-needed history of nineteenth-century nonconformity but a collection of studies of a number of personalities (primarily Congregationalists).

APPENDIX B:
A GUIDE TO PERIODICAL LITERATURE

(This is intended only as a selective guide: for a full and annotated list as of 1970 see the excellent Historical Association pamphlet, *A guide to historical periodicals in the English language*, by J. L. Kirby.)

Material on nineteenth-century British history is scattered in a plethora of periodicals. The output is so enormous and the locations so diffuse that it is almost impossible to keep in touch with everything that is published which relates to our period. Many of the specialised journals annually list articles which have appeared in the previous year and which are of interest to their readership, and some attempt a general review. (I have indicated below periodicals which undertake both these services.) The quarterly *Humanities Index* and *British Humanities Index* (which in 1962 superseded the *Subject Index to Periodicals*) are very full indexes of *all* periodical articles in the humanities. Their very comprehensiveness makes them difficult to use, but since 1976 the American Historical Association has abstracted from them *Recently Published Articles*, a check-list specifically of articles in history, including a section on the 'British Commonwealth and Ireland', which appears three times a year. Students who may occasionally wish to trace Victorian periodical-articles on a certain theme are referred to three major guides—the *Wellesley index*, the *Waterloo directory*, and the *Warwick guide to British labour periodicals, 1790–1970*. The *British Union catalogue of periodicals* details libraries which hold particular sets of periodicals.

The only periodical which confines its contents to nineteenth-century Britain is *Victorian Studies*, an interdisciplinary journal which has published important articles in historical, literary and cultural studies. It has appeared quarterly since 1957 and has a very full book-review section. One of its most important special features is the excellent annual Victorian bibliography (in the summer edition) of materials relating to the period, published in the previous year. The *Journal of British Studies*, like *Victorian Studies* a North American publication, has, since its first appearance in 1961, included many articles on the nineteenth century. There are two editions a year, and while individual books are not reviewed, the journal does occasionally include major review-articles on a particular theme.

A number of the general British historical periodicals also devote a fair amount of their space to nineteenth-century Britain. *History*, the journal of the Historical Association, appears three times a year and is directed at teachers at both school and university levels. For example, it reviews school textbooks as well as containing a large number of the usual academic book-reviews and review-articles. In this context it is also worth drawing attention to the Historical Association's *Teaching History*, a twice-yearly bulletin of developments at different levels of history teaching. The quarterly *English Historical Review*, one of the oldest and most conventional of the journals, publishes articles on all aspects of history, but with a weighting towards the medieval period. In addition to the usual book-reviews and short notices, it has an annual summary in July of the contents of other periodicals, though the list is not a comprehensive one. The *Historical Journal*, which began in 1958 with two editions a year but which now appears quarterly, leans towards modern British history. It contains fewer, but long, book-reviews as well as some excellent review-articles. The most valuable features of the twice-yearly *Bulletin of the Institute of Historical Research* are, as its title suggests, its aids to research. It includes a supplement on theses submitted and theses in progress, information on accessions and migrations of historical manuscripts, and a summary of the contents of other periodicals. The annual *Transactions of the Royal Historical Society* contains the eight papers read to the society in the previous year. *Past and Present*, bi-annual at its inception in 1951, but now quarterly was a radical reaction against the notion of studying the past for its own sake, and attempted to inject some life into historical studies by emphasising their relevance to the present. It has included some very important articles on nineteenth-century Britain, does not review individual books but contains occasional review-articles. Two English universities produce annual journals comprised mainly of articles written by their staffs—the *University of Birmingham Historical Journal* and *Renaissance and Modern Studies* (Nottingham). Last in this selection of general British periodicals is *History Today*, a monthly publication which has short, illustrated articles by specialist writers written for the general reader.

Before considering journals which specialise in certain branches of history, there are a handful of other general periodicals which deserve a brief mention. The *American Historical Review*, which appears five times a year, has the occasional important article on nineteenth-century Britain, and includes a large number of relatively short book-reviews. The *Journal of Modern History*, a quarterly on post-Renaissance history, contains a useful section of abstracts of books recently published. The *Journal of Interdisciplinary History* and the *Journal of European Studies* are both interdisciplinary quarterlies which include the occasional article on our period.

Many of the older journals discussed above mirrored historiographical developments in their early emphasis on political and contitutional and foreign and diplomatic history. As a result, the journals of politics or foreign affairs which have appeared more recently have tended to be concerned with the contemporary scene and have left the historical journals to continue their traditional work. However, major departures in historical scholarship, most notably in the branches of economic and social history, have led to the creation of periodicals in these particular areas.

One of the earliest, and undoubtedly one of the most important of these specialised journals, was the *Economic History Review* which first appeared in 1927. The current second series, begun in 1948 and published quarterly, has contained many important articles as well as the usual book-reviews. Among its most useful features are the annual 'List of publications on the economic and social history of Great Britain and Ireland', and a review of periodical literature. The thrice-yearly *Scottish Journal of Political Economy* concentrates on British economic history. Two American (the *Journal of Economic History* and *Explorations in Economic History* formerly *Explorations in Entrepreneurial History*) and one European (the *Journal of European Economic History*) general publications in the field of economic history touch upon nineteenth-century Britain only in a more desultory fashion. Of greater moment are those journals which deal with particular aspects of economic history. The *Agricultural History Review*, for example, published twice-yearly since 1953, is the principal journal in the field of British agricultural history, though its older American cousin, the quarterly *Agricultural History*, does also contain occasional articles on British agrarian history. *Business History* is the foremost periodical on British business history, but again, publications such as *Business Archives* do not totally ignore the historical aspect of the subject. Both include book-reviews and have appeared bi-annually since 1958. The illustrated quarterly *Industrial Archaeology* (formerly the *Journal of Industrial Archaeology*) was for a decade the main journal in its field, but it ceased publication in 1974. Fortunately, since 1976 a new periodical has emerged to take its place. This is the illustrated *Industrial Archaeology Review*, the journal of the Association for Industrial Archaeology. British transport history is well served by the *Journal of Transport History* (two per annum since 1953 though with a gap in the series after 1966) and the *Illustrated Transport History* (three per annum since 1968). Lastly, there are one or two very specialised economic history periodicals which the average student is unlikely to consult often, such as *Maritime History* or *Textile History*, both published annually.

Several new journals in the realm of social history have been produced in recent years, reflecting the burgeoning interest in the subject. The *Bulletin of the Society for the Study of Labour History* appeared in 1960 with the aim of collating the increasing amount of material in this particular area. It has therefore included, in addition to the usual articles and reviews, very full bibliographies of working-class history. It is published twice a year and is aimed not only at academics but at all who are interested (trade unionists, for example) in labour history. This last consideration has led some historians to eschew the formality and narrow specialism of the established journals in favour of a vehicle of more democratic appeal. Hence the establishment of *History Workshop*, a journal of socialist historians, on a bi-annual basis, in 1976. It prints very lengthy articles with a grounding in social theory, includes discussion essays, texts and documents, accounts of projects in 'people's history' (oral, community, family, etc.), and a critique of methods currently employed in the teaching of history. *Social History*, which began publication in the same year, though on a tri-annual basis, is more conventional in format. It includes articles on all periods as well as book-reviews and review-essays, and aims to reflect the stage of development which the study of social history has reached. It should not be confused with the older and important *Journal of Social History*, established in 1967 on a quarterly basis, or the *International Review of Social History* which has appeared three times a year since 1956. Both of these contain frequent articles on nineteenth-century Britain; the former also includes quite lengthy book-reviews, and the latter an annotated bibliography in each issue.

At a narrower level, oral, urban and local history all now have their own journals. *Oral History* was first published on an irregular basis in 1971 but now averages two editions a year. It includes accounts of projects in progress, many of them relating to the late nineteenth and early twentieth centuries. The *Urban History Newsletter* which Professor H. J. Dyos began in 1963 became institutionalised as the regular *Urban History Yearbook* in 1974. It contains an editorial review of the previous year's developments in urban studies, a very full bibliography of books and articles, also for the past twelve months, a review of some of the articles, and an account of research in progress. Urban historians will also find much to interest them in the *Journal of Historical Geography* (established 1975, quarterly) and the *London Journal* (also 1975, bi-annually). There are as well a number of local and regional historical journals and the published transactions of antiquarian societies, but for our purposes the only one of general interest is the quarterly *Local Historian* (formerly *Amateur Historian*).

The periodicals appertaining to the remaining sections of this bibliography can be quickly recounted. The *History of Education*, established in 1972, is the principal journal in the field of British educational history. It appears twice a year and includes a book-review section. The *Journal of Ecclesiastical History* (quarterly since 1950) fulfils the same role for religious history, although the American quarterly *Church History* also has occasional articles on our period. Wales, Scotland and Ireland each have their long-established and fairly orthodox periodicals. They are the *Welsh History Review* and the *Bulletin of the Board of Celtic Studies*, the *Scottish Historical Review*, and *Irish Historical Studies*. They all appear twice a year and include a bibliography of writings published in the previous year relating to the histories of the respective countries. Fortunately there are signs that historical scholarship in these areas is being gingered up by new publications such as the annual *Irish Social and Economic History* (since 1974) and *Llafur*, the annual journal of the Society for the Study of Welsh Labour History. Last but not least, in the realm of literary and cultural studies there are a large number of specialised periodicals (see, for example, *Nineteenth-century Fiction*, *Victorian Poetry*, the *Journal of the History of Ideas*, the *Journal of Popular Culture*, *Literature and History*, and, of course, *Victorian Studies*).

INDEX OF AUTHORS

(Numbers refer to items)

Abramsky, C. 183
Adams, W. S. 39
Adamson, J. W. 714
Adelman, P. 70, 196
Akenson, D. H. 918
Aldcroft, D. H. 392, 397, 415, 440, 444
Alderman, G. 453
Allyn, E. 130
Altick, R. D. 500, 688, 946
Amery, J. 234
Anderson, G. 558
Anderson, M. 523
Anderson, O. 69
Archer, R. L. 747
Argles, M. 759
Armstrong, A. 767
Armytage, W. H. G. 592, 711, 754
Arnold, M. 939
Arnot, R. Page 468
Arnstein, W. L. 7, 128
Ashton, E. T. 647
Ashworth, W. 391, 707
Aspinall, A. 14, 423
Atkinson, N. 919
Auchmuty, J. J. 917
Ausubel, H. 23, 73, 225

Bagehot, W. 40
Bagwell, P. S. 441, 470, 476
Bamford, T. W. 748
Banks, J. A. 525, 526
Banks, O. 526
Barker, M. 154
Barker, T. C. 442, 445
Barnard, H. C. 712
Barnett, C. 357
Bartlett, C. J. 232, 336, 363
Bauman, Z. 584
Beales, D. 20, 135
Bealey, F. 192
Beattie, A. 136
Beck, G. A. 793

Beckett, J. C. 863, 866, 870
Beer, M. 169
Beer, S. H. 137
Bell, P. M. H. 924
Beloff, M. 344
Benians, E. A. 331
Bentley, N. 488
Best, G. F. A. 295, 493
Binfield, C. A12
Binny, J. 693
Birch, R. C. 640
Black, E. C. 47, 513
Black, R. D. C. 903
Blake, R. 143, 245
Bodelsen, C. A. 341
Bolt, C. 507
Bossy, J. 792
Boultwood, M. E. A. 715, 723
Bourne, K. 306
Bowen, D. 779
Bowle, J. E. 200, 333
Boyd, A. 908
Boyle, J. W. 923
Bradley, I. 787
Bradshaw, D. C. A. 829
Branca, P. 615
Brand, C. F. 194
Brasher, N. H. 11
Breach, R. W. 386
Briggs, A. 19, 179, 180, 215, 241, 502, 602, 705
Briggs, J. H. Y. 796
Brinton, C. 201
Broadbridge, S. 451
Brock, M. 107
Brock, W. R. 60
Brockington, C. F. 675
Brose, O. 778
Brown, E. H. Phelps 478
Brown, F. K. 785
Brown, K. D. 199
Brown, L. 89

Index of Authors

Browne, H. 238
Bruce, M. 636, 639
Buchanan, R. A. 430
Buckland, P. 899, 900, 901
Buckley, J. H. 941
Bulloch, J. 860, 861
Bullock, A. 138
Bulmer-Thomas, I. 133
Burgess, K. 477
Burleigh, J. H. S. 859
Burn, W. L. 32
Burnett, J. 569
Butler, D. E. 46
Butler, J. R. M. 106
Butt, J. 506, 595, 840

Cahill, G. A. 108
Cairncross, A. K. 435
Caldwell, T. C. 349
Campbell, R. H. 413, 839, 841
Cannon, J. 97
Carrington, C. E. 332
Carr-Saunders A. M. 555
Cartwright, F. F. A8
Carty, J. 873, 874
Carus-Wilson, E. M. 395
Cazamian, L. 935
Cecil, D. 270
Cecil, G. 289
Cecil, R. 491
Chadwick, O. 765, 789
Challinor, R. 467
Chaloner, W. H. 654
Chamberlain, M. E. 326, 346
Chambers, J. D. 388, 401
Chapman, S. D. 700
Checkland, E. O. A. 668
Checkland, S. G. 250, 389, 668
Chesney, K. 687
Christensen, T. 810
Church, R. A. 393
Churchill, W. S. 239
Clapham, J. H. 380
Clapp, B. W. 387
Clark, G. S. R. Kitson, 10, 33, 286, 814
Clarke, I. F. 506
Clarke, P. F. 161
Clegg, H. A. 459
Cobbett, W. 541
Cockshut, A. O. J. 770

Cohen, E. W. 93
Cole, G. D. H. 170, 581, 582, 583, 593, 605
Cole, M. I. 188
Cole, W. A. 398
Coleman, B. I. 709
Coleman, T. 567
Collins, H. 183
Colls, R. 944
Conacher, J. B. 66, 67, 105
Connell, K. H. 913, 920
Cook, C. 45
Cooke, A. B. 72
Cookson, J. E. 59
Corfe, T. 890
Costigan, G. 216
Cotgrove, S. F. 761
Cottrell, P. L. 436
Coupland, R. 836
Court, W. H. B. 381, 385
Cowherd, R. G. 805
Cowie, E. E. 720
Cowie, L. W. 771
Cowling, M. 110, 207
Critchley, T. A. 689
Cromwell, V. 84
Crosby, T. L. 63, A2
Cross, C. 158
Crossick, G. 557
Crossley, D. W. 373
Crotty, R. D. 905
Crow, D. 607
Crowther, M. A. 780
Cullen, L. M. 904
Curl, J. S. 530
Curtis, E. 872
Curtis Jr., L. P. 538, 539, 898
Curtis, S. J. 713, 715, 723

Dangerfield, G. 38, 881
Davidoff, L. 608
Davie, G. E. 854
Davis, R. W. 122
Deane, P. 398, 399
Delgado, A. 633
Denny, A. 347
Derry, J. W. 21, 162, 233
Dessain, C. S. 790
Dicey, A. V. 86
Dixon, P. 231

Index of Authors

Dockrill, M. L. 312
Dodd, A. H. 821
Dodds, J. W. 30
Donajgrodzki, A. P. A7
Donaldson, G. 835
Donnelly Jr., J. S. 907
Douglas, R. 410
Dow, J. B. A. 841
Driver, C. 280
Drummond, A. L. 860, 861
Dunbabin, J. P. D. 551
Dunbar, J. 606
Dyos, H. J. 440, 703, 706, 710
Dyson, A. E. 722

Eaglesham, E. J. R. 745
Edsall, N. C. 665
Edwards, D. L. 782
Edwards, M. L. 797, 798
Edwards, R. D. 865, 886, 914
Eldridge, C. C. 342
Ellis, C. H. 446
Ellis, P. B. 921
Ellison, M. 418
Elman, R. M. 651
Emy, H. V. 155
Engels, F. 48, 560, 869
Ensor, R. C. K. 13
Erickson, A. B. 65, 253
Ernle, Lord 400
Evans, E. J. 409
Evans, E. W. 825, 826
Evans, H. 487
Evans, M. 487
Evans, T. 818
Everitt, A. 704
Eyck, E. 247

Fay, C. R. 378
Fearon, P. 397
Ferguson, T. 849, 850
Ferguson, W. 832
Feuchtwanger, E. J. 146, 248
Filson, A. W. 583
Finer, S. E. 678
Finlayson, G. B. A. M. 28
Fleishman, A. 937
Flinn, M. W. 377, 505, 519, 676
Foot, M. R. D. 249
Ford, B. 929

Foster, J. 577
Fox, A. 459
Franklin, T. B. 844
Fraser, D. 578, 637, 663
Fraser, P. 236
Fraser, W. H. 458
Frazer, W. M. 674
Freeman, J. 46
Fremantle, A. 189
Fried, A. 651
Frow, E. 474
Frow, R. 474
Fryer, P. 527
Fulford, R. 115
Fussell, G. E. 464

Gainer, B. 536
Gallagher, J. 347
Garnett, R. G. 598
Garrard, J. A. 535
Gartner, L. P. 534
Garvin, J. L. 234
Gash, N. 31, 62, 98, 284, 285
Gaskell, P. 848
Gauldie, E. 699
George, W. R. P. 266
Gibbon, P. 902
Gilbert, A. D. 766
Gilbert, B. B. 641
Gillespie, F. E. 173
Goldstrom, J. M. 736, 738
Gollin, A. M. 222, 274
Gosden, P. H. J. H. 573, 574, 721
Gosse, E. W. 804
Graham, G. S. 364
Gray, M. 847
Green, V. H. H. 753
Gregg, P. 375
Gregory, R. 198
Grenville, J. A. S. 323
Grigg, J. 265
Groves, R. 465
Gulley, E. E. 235
Guttsman, W. L. 49, 50
Gwyn, W. B. 113

Habakkuk, H. J. 520
Halévy, E. 3
Hall, A. R. 434
Hamburger, J. 208

Index of Authors

Hamer, D. A. 153, 166, 276, A1
Hamer, W. S. 359
Hamilton, H. 842
Hammond, B. 294, 547, 562, 563, 585
Hammond, J. L. 249, 294, 547, 562, 563, 585, 891
Handcock, W. D. 15
Hanham, H. J. 42, 99, 103, 837
Hardie, F. 80, 81
Harding, A. 691
Harris, J. 642
Harrison, A. 669
Harrison, B. 694
Harrison, J. F. C. 492, 515, 597, 763
Harrison, R. 174
Harrison, S. 422
Harrison, W. 202
Hartwell, R. M. 386, 396
Harvie, C. 210, 942
Hasbach, W. 546
Hatch, J. 345
Hawke, G. R. 450
Hay, J. R. 643
Hayes, P. 304
Heasman, K. 786
Hechter, M. 815
Henderson, P. 278
Henderson, W. O. 417
Hennock, E. P. 303
Henriques, U. R. Q. 671, 776
Herd, H. 419
Hewitt, M. 617, 621
Heyck, T. W. 167
Hibbert, C. 74
Hill, C. W. 834
Hill, R. L. 145
Hilton, G. W. 479
Himmelfarb, G. 204
Hind, R. J. 262
Hinde, W. 230
Hobsbawm, E. J. 177, 181, 383, 554
Hodgkinson, R. G. 666
Holcombe, L. 618
Hollis, P. 55, 426, 576
Horn, P. 466, 550, 565, 622
Houghton, W. E. 497
House, H. 936
Hovell, M. 599
Howard, C. H. D. 315, 316
Hudson, D. 580

Hudson, K. 429
Huggett, F. E. 51, 52
Hughes, E. 257
Hughes, M. V. 623
Hunt, E. H. 480
Hunter, J. 846
Hurst, M. 895
Hurt, J. 740
Hurwitz, E. F. 684
Hutchins, B. L. 669
Hutt, A. 456
Hyam, R. 334, 338
Hyman, R. 473
Hynes, S. L. 499

Imlah, A. H. 432
Inglis, B. 660, 909
Inglis, K. S. 812
Isichei, E. A. 803

Jackson, H. 931
Jackson, J. A. 537
James, L. 947, 948
James, R. Rhodes 71, 240, 287
Jarman, T. L. 24
Jefferys, J. B. 176, 469
Jenkins, R. 131, 218, 244
Jennings, W. I. 94, 125, 134
John, A. H. 822
Johnson, F. A. 354
Johnston, H. J. M. 533
Johnston, T. 855
Joll, J. B. 309
Jones, A. 112
Jones, D. C. 652
Jones, D. J. V. 601, 827
Jones, E. L. 403, 404, 407
Jones, G. Stedman, 579
Jones P. d'A, 811
Jones, W. D. 65, 243, 251
Judd, D. 223, 237, 283

Kamm, J. 609
Katanka, M. 474
Kauvar, G. B. 498
Kazamias, A. M. 746
Keating, P. J. 653, 938
Kee, R. 883
Keir, D. L. 41
Keith, B. 45

Index of Authors

Kellett, J. R. 708
Kelly, T. 762
Kemp, P. 369
Kennedy, F. 290
Kennedy, P. M. 362
Kent, J. 799
Kettle, A. C. 932
Kingsford, P. W. 471
Kitson Clark, G. S. R. *see* Clark
Knaplund, P. 322
Knox, H. M. 852
Koss, S. 219, 802
Kynaston, D. 172

Lambert, R. 679
Laski, H. J. 95
Lawson, J. 717
Leavis, F. R. 933
Lee, A. J. 427
Lee, J. 911
Lee, S. 213
Letwin, S. R. 205
Leventhal, F. M. 260
Levine, A. L. 414
Lewenhak, S. A6
Lewis, B. 416
Lewis, M. 370
Lewis, R. A. 677
Llewellyn, A. 29
Lochhead, M. C. 619, 620
Longford, E. 76, 297
Longmate, N. 667, 680, 695
Lovell, J. C. 461, 472
Lovelock, J. 722
Low, D. A. 337
Lowe, C. J. 311, 312, 324
Lowell, A. L. 43
Lowndes, G. A. N. 744
Lubenow, W. C. 90
Luvaas, J. 358
Lynd, H. M. 34
Lyons, F. S. L. 867, 892, 893, 896, 897
Lythe, S. G. E. 840

McBriar, A. M. 185
McBride, T. M. 566
McCaffrey, L. J. 875, 888
McCallum, R. B. 149
McCann, W. P. 725, A11
McClelland, V. A. 758

Maccoby, S. 139, 163
McCord, N. 56, 439
MacDonagh, O. 87, 92, 864
Macdonald, D. F. 4
McDowell, R. B. 142, 872, 882, 884, 912, 925
McGregor, O. R. 528
Machin, G. I. T. 61
Macintyre, A. 885
Mackay, R. F. 368
Mackenzie, J. 186
Mackenzie, N. 186
Mackie, J. D. 830
Mackintosh, J. P. 96
McLean, I. 258
McLeod, H. 769
Maclure, J. S. 719
McPherson, R. G. 728
Maehl, W. H. 109
Magnus, P. 78, 246
Maguire, W. A. 916
Malcolmson, R. W. 630
Mansergh, P. N. S. 880
Marcham, A. J. 307
Marcus, S. 561, 626
Marder, A. J. 365
Margetson, S. 631
Marlow, J. 591
Marlowe, J. 275
Marsh, D. C. 521
Marsh, P. T. 781
Marshall, D. 22, 272
Marshall, J. D. 658
Martin, Ged, 338
Martin, Graham, 942
Martin, K. 68
Marwick, W. H. 838, 856
Marx, K. 48, 869
Masterman, C. F. G. 517
Mather, F. C. 603, 690
Mathias, P. 384
Matthew, H. C. G. 157
Mayhew, H. 570, 693
Mayor, S. 813
Mechie, S. 862
Medlicott, W. N. 503
Meller, H. E. 632
Middleton, L. A3
Middleton, N. 733
Midwinter, E. C. 635, 649, 729

Miller, D. W. 928
Miller, W. R. A10
Minchinton, W. E. 408, 823
Mingay, G. E. 401, 540, 545
Mitchell, Arthur, 922
Mitchell, Austin, 150
Mitchell, B. R. 399
Mollo, B. 361
Monger, G. 317
Moody, T. W. 870, 871
Moore, D. C. 101
Moore, R. 801
Morgan, D. 116
Morgan, K. O. 160, 259, 267, 819
Morley, J. 529
Morrell, W. P. 339, 340
Morris, A. J. A. 168, 314
Morris, H. L. 102
Morris, J. 343
Morris, J. H. 824
Morris, M. 175
Morris, R. J. 681
Morrish, I. 716
Morton, A. L. 594
Mowat, C. L. 264, 645
Murphy, B. 374
Murphy, J. 739, 742
Musgrave, P. W. 718
Musson, A. E. 457, 460

Neal, T. A. 25
Neale, R. S. 575
Neff, W. F. 614
Newman, J. H. (Cardinal) 757
Newsome, D. 750, 788
Nicholls, D. 784
Nicolson, H. G. 79
Norman, E. R. 777, 794, 868, 926, 927
Nossiter, T. J. 123
Nowell-Smith, S. H. 37
Nowlan, K. B. 879

O'Brien, C. C. 894
O'Farrell, P. 876, 877
Ogilvie, V. 749
O'Leary, C. 114
Olney, R. J. 124
d'Ombrain, N. 355
Orwin, C. S. 402
Ostrogorski, M. 132

Owen, D. 644
Page Arnot, R. *see* Arnot
Pankhurst, E. S. 118
Parris, H. 88, 91
Payne, P. L. 412
Peacock, A. J. 552
Pearsall, R. 496, 508, 624, 625
Pearson, M. 629
Pelling, J. 26, 120, 140, 182, 190, 192, 195, 455
Penson, L. M. 308
Percival, A. C. 751
Perkin, H. 481, 495
Perry, P. J. 405, 406
Petrie, C. A. 263, 296, 486
Pfautz, H. W. 650
Phelps Brown, E. H. *see* Brown
Pierson, S. 184
Pike, E. R. 509, 510, 511, 512
Pimlott, J. A. R. 634
Pinchbeck, I. 616, 621
Pinto-Duschinsky, M. 292
Plamenatz, J. 209
Platt, D. C. M. 330, A5
Poirier, P. P. 191
Pollard, H. M. 724
Pollard, S. 373, 411, 572, 596
Pollins, H. 452
Porter, B. 335, 352
Postgate, R. 582
Poynter, J. R. 659
Prest, J. 288
Price, R. 353
Prothero, R. E. *see* Ernle
Pryde, G. S. 831

Quinault, R. 588

Radzinowicz, L. 692
Ramelson, M. 610
Read, D. 35, 36, 121, 242, 421, 589
Reader, W. J. 490, 556
Reardon, B. M. G. 772
Redford, A. 379, 531
Reed, M. C. 449
Reid, J. H. S. 193
Rempel, R. A. 148
Rhodes James, R. *see* James
Rich, E. E. 741
Richards, D. A9

Index of Authors

Richardson, H. W. 392
Richter, M. 211
Ridley, J. 282
Ripley, B. 467
Rix, M. 428
Robbins, K. 256
Robbins, M. 445, 448
Roberts, B. C. 461, 462
Roberts, D. 638
Roberts, R. 701, 702
Robinson, R. 347
Robson, R. 53
Robson, W. A. 302
Roderick, A. J. 817
Roderick, G. W. 760
Rodgers, B. 657
Roebuck, J. 483
Rolo, P. J. V. 229
Rose, M. E. 662, 664
Rosen, A. 119
Rostow, W. W. 382
Rover, C. 117, 611
Rowbotham, S. 612
Rowland, P. 159, 268
Royle, E. 164, 165
Rubinstein, D. 696
Rudé, G. 554
Russell, R. C. 553
Ryder, J. 482

Salt, J. 596
Samuel, R. 549, 568
Sanderson, M. 755, 756
Saul, S. B. 394, 433
Saunders, L. J. 851
Savage, C. I. 442
Saville, J. 178, 179, 180, 532
Sayers, R. S. 390
Scharf, A. 942
Schlote, W. 431
Schurman, D. M. 372
Schuyler, R. L. 328
Scotland, J. 853
Seaman, L. C. B. 9
Searle, G. R. 212
Seldon, A. 655
Sellers, I. 796
Semmel, B. 329, 351, 800
Seton-Watson, R. W. 305
Seymour, C. 100

Shannon, R. 27
Shaw, A. G. L. 325
Shock, M. 138
Silver, H. 482, 717, 726, 727
Simey, M. B. 648
Simmons, J. 443, 447
Simon, B. 734, 735
Slaven, A. 843
Smellie, K. B. 6, 44, 300
Smelser, N. J. 522
Smith, A. 783
Smith, E. A. 14
Smith, F. B. 111
Smith, P. 147, 293
Smout, T. C. 505, 833
Solow, B. L. 906
Soloway, R. 806
Somervell, D. C. 203, 485
Sorensen, G. C. 498
Southgate, D. 144, 151, 281
Spinner, T. 252
Spring, D. 543
Stafford, A. 475
Stansky, P. 85, 156
Stedman Jones, G. *see* Jones
Steele, E. D. 887
Steiner, Z. S. 318, A4
Stephen, L. 213
Stephens, M. D. 760
Stevenson, J. 588
Stewart, R. 64
Stewart, W. A. C. 725
Strauss, E. 878
Sturgis, J. L. 227
Sturt, M. 731
Sutherland, G. 83, 730, 743
Symon, J. A. 845
Symondson, A. 775

Tames, R. 376
Tarn, J. N. 697, 698
Tate, G. 171
Taylor, A. J. 82, 656
Taylor, A. J. P. 217, 313
Taylor, R. 291
Temperley, H. 683
Temperley, H. W. V. 308, 320
Terrot, C. 628
Thal, H. van 214
Tholfsen, T. R. 586

Index of Authors

Thomas, B. 820
Thomas, J. A. 126, 127
Thomas, M. W. 670
Thomis, M. I. 564, 661
Thompson, A. F. 459
Thompson, D. 604
Thompson, D. M. 795
Thompson, E. P. 277, 559, 571
Thompson, F. 548
Thompson, F. M. L. 542
Thompson, P. 197, 279, 494
Thomson, D. 5
Thornhill, W. 301
Thornley, D. 889
Thornton, A. P. 350
Tillotson, K. 934
Tobias, J. J. 685, 686
Tranter, N. 518
Trevelyan, G. M. 8, 226, 255, 484
Tribe, D. 224
Trotter, W. P. 371
Trudgill, E. 627
Tsuzuki, C. 261
Tuathaigh, G. O. 910
Turberville, A. S. 129
Turner, B. 438
Turner, H. A. 463
Tylecote, M. 764

Uzoigwe, G. N. 348

Vicinus, M. 613, 943
Vincent, J. 72, 152

Walmsley, R. 590
Walsh, W. 930
Ward, J. T. 254, 516, 544, 587, 600, 672, 673
Ward, W. R. 768
Wardle, D. 732
Watkin, E. I. 791
Watson, G. 206
Watteville, H. de 360
Wearmouth, R. F. 807, 808, 809
Webb, B. 298, 299, 454

Webb, R. K. 1, 945
Webb, S. J. 299, 454
Webster, C. K. 319, 321
Weitzmann, S. 733
West, E. G. 737
Whetham, E. H. 402
White, R. J. 57, 58, 141, 489
Wickwar, W. H. 424
Wiener, J. H. 310, 425, 514
Wilkinson, R. 752
Willey, B. 773, 774
Williams, D. 816, 828
Williams, E. E. 682
Williams, F. 420
Williams, J. B. 437
Williams, L. J. 824
Williams, R. 940
Williams, T. D. 914
Williamson Jr., S. R. 356
Wilson, A. 858
Wilson, J. 228
Wilson, P. A. 555
Wilson, R. G. 413, 544
Winks, R. W. 327
Winter, J. 269
Wolfe, W. 187
Wolff, M. 706
Wood, A. 2
Woodham-Smith, C. 77, 915
Woodroofe, K. 646
Woodward, E. L. 12, 367
Woodward, J. A9
Wootton, G. 54
Wrench, J. E. 273
Wright, D. G. 104
Wright, L. C. 857
Wrigley, E. A. 524

Yeo, E. 571
Young, A. F. 647
Young, G. M. 15, 17, 18, 504
Young, K. 220

Zebel, S. H. 221
Ziegler, P. 75, 271

Ref
Z
2019
N5
1978

SEP 19 1979